The Magic of Noticing

The Magic of Noticing

Buddhism in our Modern World

Andy Spragg

Sapientiam Publishing

Sapientiam Publishing

The Sangha House,
First Floor
Mitre House
Tower Street
Taunton
United Kingdom
TA1 4BH
www.thesanghahouse.co.uk

Contents

Chapter 1. Foreword

I came to Buddhism about 25 years ago. I had suffered with a tumour in my hip joint at quite a young age (21) and the shock of this really made me think about my life and my spirituality. I started to reach out and look at religions to fill the gap. To an extent they all seemed to be telling me how to think. Yes, they told me how to behave but primarily for me it felt as if I must think in a certain way and practice my spirituality in a certain way. Then, I found a beginners' guide to Buddhism in a second-hand bookshop and this took my life forward. I am also a Tai Chi teacher and I discovered Tai Chi a little earlier. But my Tai Chi eventually became a key part of my Buddhist practice as there is so much synergy between the two.

For many years I worked in information technology as a project and programme manager. But gradually I realised that I had a desire to teach from my experience of studying both Meditation and Tai Chi. My wife, Denise, and I now run a successful Buddhist based health and wellbeing centre in Taunton, Somerset, UK - The Sangha House (www.thesanghahouse.co.uk)

Chapter 2. Introduction

My experience of studying and then teaching Buddhism here in the UK has revealed three main perceptions about Buddhism in the west.

The first is that there still seems to be this impression that you must become a monk to become a Buddhist; that you must give up everything you own and live in a cave or live a monastic life. The second impression is that many people are nervous of this word "spiritual". It carries many connotations and implies a hippy-like religion, perhaps. Therefore, Buddhism gets left alone by many people who perhaps feel a sense of fear towards it. Perhaps they don't see how it could fit in with their modern life.

The third is that Buddhist meditation is in some way a therapy. It is used when we are depressed or anxious. When we are not, we can forget about it and crack on with our busy lives.

So, my purpose in writing this book is to demonstrate first of all that the teachings of the Buddha are actually very grounded in nature and full of common sense. They are not magical or esoteric. That they very much belong and can form part of our modern western society. That the practices that Buddhism encourages should not be seen as a religion; more a way or approach to life and something that we should all apply to some level, even when we are feeling healthy and strong.

If we look at the physical aspect of health, we understand that we don't wait until we have a cold or the flu to take up jogging. In fact, we should not. We take it up when we are feeling strong enough and healthy enough to do so. In this way, we get fitter and stronger and are better able to fight off the cold and the flu. The same applies with the mental aspect. We practise when we are strong so that we can cope with the complex curveballs that life throws at us.

Many people come to Buddhism with one key question arising. Is Buddhism a religion, a philosophy, an approach to life? What is it? This book will allow you to draw your own conclusion to this. My personal view is that Buddhism can and does include all of these areas and excludes none. It is very much a personal choice. You make Buddhist practice yours!

There is a key word there. Practice. However you approach Buddhism, you are going to need to practise. Here, we are, of course, talking about mindfulness and meditation. We are going to find out, in this book, why this practice is so important.

When I was a young boy, I loved magic - magic tricks. Magic fascinated me. Over the years I became rather scientific and was really interested in the debunking of magic. Wanting to understand how the magician "did it". Now, I have come to realise that I really do not want to know how everything works. It is now, important to me that there is still magic out there.

I think what led me to this place was a letting go, as part of my Buddhist practice. Seeing now, how that scientific mind of mine worked, I understand that it was a desire to control things; to control the chaos of the world. I had a belief that the world is chaotic but if we understood enough about it, we could control it.

Buddhist practice has led me to a place where I can understand the beauty in that chaos, see how it teaches me and delivers to me a deep acceptance of the way things are. Letting go of anger and frustration in my life has been one of the biggest benefits I have gained from my practice.

Magic is a wonderful word. It has associated with it connotations of mystery and somehow conjures up a sense of spirituality somehow.

I see two types of magic in this world. The type that gets featured in Harry Potter – "quick magic." This is the magic that is most commonly sought after. This isn't the magic that I am talking about here. I'm talking about the second type - slow magic. This magic is perceivable by all of us and is right in front of our own eyes.

Let me give you an example. A branch falls off a tree. The green leaves on it start to wither and die. It will soon be brown and dead. The scientists will tell us that the lack of water and nutrients flowing through the branch have led to its death. But if we now pump water and nutrients into that dead wood, it won't come back to life. Something else is missing. This thing called life, and what that is, we don't really know. What, actually, is life? This is the slow magic.

This is what Buddhist practice is about. Investigating our direct experience of life, taking what we find, accepting things as they are. Taking a deep interest in our world without expectation, judgement and with compassion and equanimity. (I'll come to equanimity, in detail, later)

The Magic of Noticing – Andy Spragg

If you start to practise this stuff you will probably fairly quickly notice that all you have to do is notice some aspect of your experience and it changes. For example, if you have fear in your life, if you focus on the physical sensation of fear instead of allowing your mind to focus on the thoughts around the thing you are fearing, the fear fades.

If you start to notice the way you make assumptions about a total stranger, the first time you meet them, the assumptions will fade.

But we have to notice first and, actually, that is all we have to do.

Interestingly, the emotions and ways of thinking that we would describe as wholesome, grow when we notice them, whereas the unwholesome things fade.

Fear, anger, envy, these types of things fade. But if when we meet a good friend, we pay close attention to our heart area and feel the compassion and friendship there like a warm smile in that area, it grows!

Going deeper, it is possible that the touch of a conscious mind affects things in our universe. There is some fascinating work going on in the field of quantum mechanics that seems to back this up. When quantum particles are observed, they change their nature. How can that work?

As we deepen our meditation practice, we notice this behaviour. The deeper we take our interest, the more our relationship with the object deepens and reveals itself. Our primary focus is us. It is inward. Into our minds and our bodies. The deeper we go with this noticing, the more our nature is revealed to us. Take frustration for example. When frustration arises, we quite naturally focus on the thing that frustrates us. Then we start to think about this thing and that thinking takes the form of justification. The mind argues its position for feeling frustrated. It is like having a friend who is bitter about something someone has done to them and will not shut up and let go of it. Even when the other person has long since left the scene, area or even the country!

Now, if we just notice, we start to see first of all that we are frustrated. Sometimes these emotions have to be really noisy to us because our lives are so busy. As our practice develops, we start to notice frustration appearing a great deal earlier. We start to notice the manifestation of it in our bodies - the tension that comes in. Then we also start to notice the dialogue in the mind that accompanies it. We hear the justifications coming in as if they are that bitter friend. Next, we start to notice that although the frustration is still there, it feels less personal. We are aware of it, but it is just another sense experience, like a bad smell or a loud sound. Then we start to accept it - accepting that just like the loud noise, it is just a part of life. Frustration itself can't hurt us. It is just a sense experience. Lastly the frustration evaporates. Just like the bad smell or the loud noise will. Other frustrations will come but the magic is in the noticing. The more we spend our life in the present moment, the more we notice our reactions to life and soften into it, the less the things that cause us frustration and suffering in life, will hurt us.

The Magic of Noticing – Andy Spragg

Chapter 3. History of Buddhism – the historical Buddha

It is very useful to see where Buddhism came from. It really illustrates the main reasons why the practice has developed the way it has.

This is a little challenging however because digging into the historical Buddha is difficult. There is very little written about his actual life. Most writing that describes the Buddha describes his teachings. There is very little written about him as a person.

What we do know is that he was an ordinary man. He was not a mystical being, although his story is quite extraordinary. He was born an Indian prince around 500 BC. He was born in the region of Lumbini which was a small area in what is now Nepal. His father was a chieftain in a clan called the Shakya.

His early life was extremely privileged. He needed nothing and his father clearly had desires for his son to inherit his title. His father's name was Suddhodana. The Buddha's name was Siddhartha Gautama. His mother died shortly after his birth; her name was Maya. The history is vague, but it is said that a seer came to visit at the moment of his birth, as this was the tradition of noble families. his name was Asita. He foretold that there would be two paths for this child: either he would become a great warlord, or he would become a great religious leader. Gautama's father clearly wanted him to inherit his title and to become a great warlord, so he set out to protect and educate Gautama to ensure he was brought up in the way of a prince. A part of this practice was to ensure that the prince never saw any sign of suffering in the world. Sick or elderly servants were banned from the palace. Maybe his father realised that if the Buddha saw the realities of life, he would start to question it. But of course, that is exactly what the Buddha did.

At the age of 16 his father arranged his marriage to Yashodhara his cousin and they had a son Rahula. It is clear that he did love his wife and his son very much, but his destiny took him on a different path.

The Buddha had a charioteer whose name was Channa. Channa was very loyal to the Buddha and one day at the age of 29 Gautama asked if he could leave the palace against his father's wishes. The story tells that he left on three separate occasions and for the first time he saw old age, sickness and death. The lack of understanding here crashed down on him. He was an intelligent man, but he could not reconcile this. What was life's purpose? If we all get sick, age and die, what is the purpose of life? In India at the time there was an extremely strong tradition and practice of ascetism. Ascetics were held in high regard and there were many of them living in the forests. Essentially the main goal of the practice was to free the soul from the earthly body through extreme hardship, malnourishment and self-harm. The aim was to drive the spirit out of the body. Siddhartha Gautama chose to join them and in his 29th year he rode out deep in to the forest. The Pali Canon (the Buddhist "Bible") describes the different teachers he met. He became extremely single minded and mentally strong, and very quickly established himself as a very strong practitioner. Within the forest other ascetics saw him as their leader, so strong had his practice become, and they started to travel with him. For seven years he studied. Over time the practice took its toll and he became very physically weak but very mentally strong through the practice of meditation.

But it was not delivering the answer he sought. This stage of his life ended when he was bathing in a river. He was so physically weak he very nearly drowned. Luckily a young girl was passing, and she helped him out of the river and gave him some milk and honey. When his ascetic friends heard of this, they left him in disgust as they felt he had deserted them. The Buddha now realised that this was not the correct path. It was going to kill him before he found his answer. So, the Buddha resolved to settle down under a tree in meditation and to meditate until he had his answer - until he understood life. This is what led him to his approach to resolving suffering and then to teaching across Northern India for the next 45 years. The Buddha delivered his first sermon just outside the modern town of Varanasi in a place called Sarnath. The first people to attend were those very ascetics that had worked with him for all those years in the forests. Because of this I believe the Buddha concentrated on suffering as the central theme of his first sermon, because their main practice in those forests has centred around suffering. Many people that come to Buddhism find it a little depressing because it sounds like it will be all about understanding suffering. This isn't the case. Buddhism had as its first sermon a focus on suffering purely because of the experiences of that first audience; because of the work and the suffering that they had gone through with the Buddha. Buddhism is about compassion it is about connection and yes, it is about freedom from suffering. This book is going to explain why.

The Magic of Noticing – Andy Spragg

3.1   The spread of Buddhism

After the Buddha's death, Buddhism spread through South East Asia, from its root in India. Over a period of about 600 years It travelled to Tibet, China, Sri Lanka, Thailand and Japan. The nature of the practice changed but the fundamentals of the spirituality always remained. Mindfulness, meditation and compassion, working towards the alleviation of suffering in oneself and others. Because of cultural influences, these different locations developed very different varieties of Buddhism. Indian is gentle and simple in its approach, Chan (from China), is quite disciplined. Zen (from Japan), even more so. Tibetan is ritualistic and contains some esoteric practices influenced by shamanism which was prevalent in Tibet when Buddhism arrived. The major influence that led to these variations was culture. Pour the raw spiritual approach into that culture-container and it takes the shape of that container.

The Magic of Noticing – Andy Spragg

Chapter 4. Introducing Buddhist practice

Buddhist thinking largely focuses on the nature of mind. It should be stressed that this is not neuroscience. It is not about the brain; it is about our human experience of the mind and although there are overlaps, the two are inherently different. When we focus on mind, we are talking about our own experience of our own mind.

You can think of this in a similar way to your experience of driving a car. Let us imagine you have never learnt to drive. But you take a mechanics course, become proficient and this enables you to be able to strip the car down to its component parts and put it back together again. You even have the ability to fix the car, solving problems. But even with this knowledge, you cannot drive.

So, the knowledge of the brain does not give you the direct experience of Mind. Just like knowing how the accelerator works, allows you to explain why the car goes faster when you press on the pedal, it still does not reveal to you the experience of driving if you've never driven.

Buddhist thinking is not really interested in how the brain works (although it IS interesting). It is interested in the experience of mind and how this nature of mind affects our life.

Mind is also more than brain. In meditation we often take our awareness down into the body. We can take our awareness right down into our big toe. Placing our mind literally into our big toe. Of course, straight away questions start to come up. Is Mind awareness? Where is Mind? What is Mind? All interesting questions and really good ones to ask in meditation.

The Magic of Noticing – Andy Spragg

4.1   Why is Buddhism all about Mind?

This is really our starting point. You soon discover that Buddhism is all about Mind. You may hear of rituals, religious devotions, incense, statues and many other aspects that go into the melting pot of Buddhism. But sitting below it all, driving it all, is the self-study of the mind.

In order to understand why, we take ourselves back to the Buddha and what he had experienced in the forests during his seven years as an ascetic. The essence of the ascetic's practice was to drive the soul out of the body. The Buddha realised that this was fundamentally wrong. He even deliberately turned his back on a practice centred on the soul, the very thing the ascetic practice was trying to drive out. He did not deny it. He just decided to investigate the idea with an open mind, essentially, to see if he could find a soul through meditation.

He went back to what he was trying to investigate in the first place. What is the purpose of life if we all get sick, get old and die? He realised that, obviously, we can't escape these three factors, but we can escape suffering itself. His answer was remarkably simple.

We don't suffer because of the things that happen to us; we suffer because of our reaction to the things that happen to us.

This startlingly simple idea is at the root of everything we practise in Buddhism.

It was this, that the Buddha set out to explore and then teach and he did so to great depth.

That reaction, itself, is all about mind. How our mind reacts to things. It is this that the Buddha understood, and this is why Buddhism was recently referred to by HH The Dalai Lama as a science of the mind.

But of course, although the idea sounds simple, actually changing our reaction is a huge task. Just think about the last time you got angry. It's easy to think "well, I'll just count to 10, take a deep breath and calm down". But life is not like that. It delivers some phenomenal judgements and miscarriages of justice on us, almost every day, when we are not expecting them and however much we may hide our feelings with a smile, we are suffering inside.

So, let us dig into this. But before, we delve into how we fix the problem, we need understand the nature of the problem to be fixed! The first section is all about Buddhist thinking in this area. Why we react the way we do and what the challenges are.

To answer this question of why it is all about mind, we are going to delve into this a little and look at the Buddha's fundamental view; that we don't suffer because of the things that happen to us, we suffer because of our reaction to the things that happen to us.

Remember that we always, with Buddhist practice, look for direct experience. We do not work with doctrine. We do not believe simply because we are told. We go and find out for ourselves and we do this through meditation. We have a vehicle to work with - this aspect of Mind that allows mind to see itself. We call this part of the mind The Gardener (Section 4.4 for further details about this).

With meditation we work through three fields of mindfulness; the body, the mind and our sense of self.

Where does our suffering come from? And how do we let it go? How do we truly let go of our reactions to things?

We could say that it is inevitable that if something bad happens to us, we are bound to suffer, and this can manifest as fear and anxiety. Even in our more confident moments we sometimes feel a level of disquiet. It is obvious, right? Of course, if something happens to us, we are going to react with fear, anger or another go-to emotion? Well, it is this we investigate with meditation and mindfulness. We explore to see if that is actually the case. Again, with Buddhism, we take nothing at face value. We explore and investigate.

I often say that in order to accept something and let it go, we have to take hold of it first. To let go of a ball, we have to have it in our hand first.

The same applies here to the things that cause us suffering. It is certainly true that things are going to happen to us. We cannot wrap ourselves in cotton wool. So, the only thing we can work on is the reactions which usually manifest as emotional content itself. E.g. fear and anxiety.

4.2   Working with the five senses

But we have to start somewhere, and we need to start simple. Buddhism is extremely experiential. The Buddha encouraged us not to take anything told to us by others at face value. His instruction was for us to go and find out for ourselves. This was his approach, that he found delivered his understanding and in his teaching he was encouraging us to do the same. He even advised that we do not take what he was teaching at face value. We are to go out and find out for ourselves!

The starting point is how we connect with the world around us. Our direct contact with the world is with the five senses we have. So, this is where we start.

All our sense experiences go through the same path. I should just emphasize again that this is not neuroscience or physiology. It is about our experiences of how the senses work.

The sense trigger touches the sense object. Every sense has a trigger. A chemical enters the nose and triggers the sense of smell. The experience then passes through a path through the mind. Associated with each sensory system is what we call the sense door. This is the first part of the mind that notices the sensation. At this point the process is entirely unconscious. We are not yet aware of the sensory experience. Next, the mind makes a very quick choice. It decides between like, dislike or neutral to the experience. Again, here, this is usually beneath our conscious perception. Up till now, we are unaware of the sense experience. Now the full power of the mind engages and kicks in. It embellishes the experience, drawing on all of our life experience to justify the choice.

All these steps are entirely individual to us. The nature of our mind, all its experiences and the influence of our lives all pile in to give each and every one of us a slightly different experience. Just think of Marmite™! Some of us love it and some of us hate it.

The Magic of Noticing – Andy Spragg

But we have a further complication in Buddhist thinking. A sixth sense. Mind. OK, so I might know what you are thinking. Sixth sense? Can we read minds? Can we see the future? No! In Buddhist thinking, we just have the understanding that the mind has its trigger just the same as our other sense organs do, and this goes through exactly the same process. The trigger is a mental object such as a thought. Just as a chemical enters the nose and triggers the sense of smell, a thought or mental object enters the mind and triggers the mind sensory organ. We can no more stop a thought entering the mind than stop a chemical entering the nose. But we don't have to pay attention to it! If you think of smells, for example, if we are listening to a piece of music or enjoying the feel of the wind across your skin, at that point you are not noticing the smell entering your nose. We can take exactly the same approach with mind and with thoughts. We do not have to pay attention to them.

It is remarkable that the Buddha figured all this out just through observation. This whole process happens in a split second. But we can, too! If we learn to meditate, we can become consciously aware of this process, earlier on in the whole cycle. Becoming aware of the first moment that Mind is triggered by the sense door and the subsequent embellishment by Mind itself.

4.3   Dealing with thoughts

Many people when they come to meditation express a concern that they cannot shut up their minds.

This is where our challenge is. Because we seem to have a tendency to believe that our thoughts are somehow "me". Or that if we do not pay attention to our thoughts, we somehow cannot function. Anyone who meditates soon discovers that this is not the case. Life happens whether or not we pay attention to our thoughts! We also start to understand how our minds sometimes even tell lies! In this way, through this noticing, our thoughts lose their power over us.

Through meditation we seek to take away the power of thought and see behind it.

So, here is another analogy for you which can help. We can view Mind like layers of the sea. The top layer is where the larger thoughts roll around, like large waves and these, we feel, have a great deal of power over us. This is the noisy layer. The waves are powerful. I like to call these thoughts, these big waves, the juggernaut thoughts. When they occur, they take us over. They may be unimportant, but we listen to them. "I wonder what's for dinner tonight?". Often, they come in the form of internal dialogue in the mind. The mind chats to itself, justifies, argues, judges and explains.

The next layer below it is the foam. Here we have tiny little thoughtlets forming all the time. Snippets of conversations, little bits of music, a memory of a face. Often in this layer, the mental objects arise as images or sound. So, they are more akin to sensory experiences. This layer is, essentially, our entry point into the subconscious.

Then, below this, we have pure mind. With practice, we can reach this layer. But in order to reach it, we have to accept that the top two layers exist and are not going to go away. If we do not accept the nature of mind, we will never reach that quiet, still place, because the mind will not quieten. The waves on top of the ocean are there whether we like them or not. Once we start to accept that they are there, we can let them go; ignore them, if you like.

The mind is not a calm, logical place. It is complex and it is chaotic. We call it "monkey mind", leaping from branch to branch in a random fashion. This is exactly the behaviour of Mind. If you strive to get your mind to stop doing this, you will fail. That's what minds do. The aim of meditation is to develop an accepting approach to Mind - to let it do its thing while you focus awareness on the meditation subject. Slowly the mind will respond and sink and settle. But you cannot "make" it do that.

Actually, we should not try to lose that chaotic nature of Mind. It is out of this chaos that our wonderful individuality and our incredible creativity come from. We should embrace its chaotic nature. That is just the way it is!

4.4   The three aspects of our mind

Here we have a piece of Buddhist thinking which, again, is not neuroscience but it is a very good and helpful way to view Mind. A model, if you like. We study this with our direct internal experience. Essentially, taking our awareness inside to look at the mind and its nature. It really is phenomenal that we can all do this.

Mind can be seen as having three parts to it.

1. Manas. The thinking part of the mind. The part you are most familiar with. It thinks, it worries, it plans, it schemes, it regrets etc. (Manas is a Pali word. Pali was the ancient

language that the Buddha and his disciples spoke. Many of our Buddhist words are Pali translations.)

2. The Store Consciousness. It remembers. But it is more than just the picture book memory we think of. It consists of both mind and body. Everything that has happened to us (and perhaps to our ancestors?) exists in here. Even the injuries that have happened to our body form part of our store consciousness.

3. The Gardener. The most important part of this trio and key to the practice of mindfulness. This is the part of the mind that can sit and watch the other two at work. Our pure awareness. It can watch the manas draw on the store consciousness, make conclusions, imagine, embellish etc. Later on, we will find out why this watcher of the mind is called the Gardener.

So, that process we outlined earlier in section 4.2. Sensory objects and their flow? The Gardener is able to watch all this at work. To see how the mind reacts. To see it make its choices and see how it embellishes with remembering and thinking. All of this creates new mental objects which, low and behold are all sensory triggers for that sixth sense of ours, Mind itself!

This is an incredibly complex process that we can now watch with fascination - the real heart of mindfulness, and the reason for mindfulness, if you like. When our practice deepens it is an amazing discovery to see how we can watch our own minds at work. To notice the way our thoughts and emotions drive us. How our internal bias and habitual thinking colours and changes the world. How we react to things that we see as challenging and then start to notice that, in reality, they do not challenge us. The

The Magic of Noticing – Andy Spragg

Gardener part of the mind gives us all of this. In meditation we get in touch with this patient watcher of the mind.

4.5   Working with emotions

If we are going to make progress with meditation, we have to learn to deal with emotions. Emotions are the strongest way we react to the things that happen to us and they affect us to many degrees.

We can view emotions as being made up of three parts:

1. The first is the most familiar to us - the thoughts. When we experience emotion, our mind justifies the way we are feeling. This often occurs in the form of our internal dialogue. "It's not surprising I'm angry, he did that to me" and so on. This justification and judging that goes on then fuels the emotion and grows it. In this way, our ego is convincing itself that it is right to be feeling this way.
2. The energy of the emotion. This is felt in the body. It is the raw experience of the emotion, felt in the heart and the gut. The strong emotions come with a great deal of physical tension in the body. After the emotion has melted away, we are often left with the after-effects in the body, such as aches, pain and exhaustion.
3. Action. The result of our emotion, generally some action materializes from the way we are feeling. From the simple way we hold ourselves to full-blown expressions of anger or fear. This is the part that makes our emotions visible to the world.

All emotions appear in the body. The mind does the thinking, the body does the feeling. So, in Buddhist practice, it is the physical energy that we get in touch with. When feeling emotion, we stay away from the thought, the justification and the judgement. This will simply make the emotion increase. Instead, we draw our awareness to the physical energy and study its nature. Asking ourselves, where is it in the body we can feel the emotion and what does it feel like. No matter what emotion is being experienced, this is how we approach it.

Initially this may prove difficult. All through our life we have been paying attention to the thoughts we have. We listen to their strong justifications as they seem to justify the emotions we are feeling. But just imagine for a moment, a dog's relationship with its emotions. It doesn't have our huge gift of language. It doesn't even know what the emotions are called! All the dog can do is feel the emotion. It can't justify, explain or understand the emotion. All it can do is experience.

We try to keep that practice present all the time, staying steadily mindful of our body and keeping vigilant for emotional tension. When it arises, we focus on stepping into it with gentle softness and friendship, physically releasing that emotional tension. The more we can practice with this, even when we aren't meditating, the more this will become a habit. A habit of gentle observation. We are going to have to apply tenacity here, but the good news is, as we develop this into habit, the easier it will get to do it. Use habit. Form habit. Habit is your ally.

But we haven't fully grasped the problem yet. We now feel the effect of the world on the physical being, but we need now need to see why. As a slight aside, there is something startlingly simply that has emerged here. Often, in Buddhist practice we talk about connecting more deeply with the world around us. Well, this

The Magic of Noticing – Andy Spragg

illustrates exactly how that happens. Stuff happens in the world and you feel a direct physical response deep in your heart! No disconnection. Full connection.

4.6   Why do we suffer?

So, we have now started to feel our emotional response to the world, but we still do not actually know why we suffer? Buddhist thinking says that this occurs because of Mind - the thinking mind. This mind has an ego. A sense of self. This sense of self is not representative of the way the world actually is. It creates a picture of a sense of separation from the universe. There is "I" and there is everything else. This sense of I seeks to constantly protect itself from perceived risk. Threats to it are displayed as our aversion; if it perceives things that it believes will enforce it and make it stronger, these are represented as desires. Buddhism gives us a vehicle for exploring these effects on us called the Worldly Winds. They are pairings of things, and there are four of them. If you look into the things that cause you suffering you will find their origins in these pairings or in a combination of them. We will look into this subject in more detail later in the book, but for now, the basic pairings are pleasure versus pain, gain versus loss, praise versus blame and fame versus infamy. These pairings either feed our ego and make it feel safe and nourished or they threaten the ego and make it feel fear and diminished in nature. So, our ego, or our thinking mind, responds by wanting to wrap itself with a view of a static world which does not change. We know the worldly winds are out there affecting us. If we could keep away everything that threatens us, then perhaps we can keep ourselves free from the emotional reactions that come with the Worldly Winds. But now,

The Magic of Noticing – Andy Spragg

having experienced change and its inevitability, we have directly felt that it is impossible to keep everything away. These winds will always reach us in some way, shape or form.

The only way to find true stillness and tranquillity we seek is to step away from our normal mind; a mind that jumps from subject to subject, is full of critique and judgement and is far from still. We need to get in touch with the Gardener, that part of the mind which sits and watches everything. This awareness is there all the time and has the capability of watching everything at work, seeing the thinking mind as it struggles to protect itself, as it strives to resist the worldly winds and triggers the emotional turmoil in the body.

4.7   The roots of suffering

What are the roots of our suffering, underlying everything we suffer for?

The Buddha discovered that all of our suffering originates from these three human reactions.

Desire – the grasping, wanting nature.

Aversion – When we push away things we do not like, hatred, ill will etc all come from this

Delusion - the mind's behaviour of creating an artificial veil in front of the world as it is. The trickiest one of all!

Gently, with practice, we are establishing a habit of noticing all this ego protection that goes on and slowly we allow ourselves to let go of this.

The Magic of Noticing – Andy Spragg

This book will take you through a whole series of approaches and techniques to notice these states arising and soften their power.

4.7.1 Desire

Of course, it is very human of us to try to chase after the things we like. Or to keep them once we have them. In Buddhist practice, we are not saying that we have to give up everything we like! The practice is about starting to understand the nature of desire in the mind. To feel its pull. So that we can stay present, grounded, mindful. We do practice renunciation in Buddhism but this is so that we can really illustrate to us the difference between true physical need and desire. Often the desiring mind will chase after things that aren't actually wholesome for us!

Our desire has evolved in us for hundreds if not thousands of generations. We would not have lasted long as a species without it. But the mind does not always deliver up what we really need. The minds sense of self or ego will chase things that it believes will nourish it and in our modern world, with all the potential sensory pleasures we have out there, it sometimes gets it wrong. Just think of alcoholism or drug abuse as examples of this.

By starting to notice the power of desire on our mind, feeling its pull and seeing directly what is pulling it, we can stay centred and make better choice about the desire in our lives.

4.7.2 Aversion

Aversion is anything we try to push away or avoid in our life.

Aversion is not a bad thing. It helps us see danger and teaches us to protect ourselves. The problem is, we have become so good at doing it, we do not often see the positives. We have a great day, meet lovely people, see lovely things and one bad thing happens and we focus on that.

Let's look at the physical side first. In fact, all different types of aversion have an effect in the body. Often, the body tells us we are reacting to something even before the mind is consciously aware! Some of our aversions are very deep seated and may go back, in terms of their origin, for many years.

The real antidote to aversion is compassion and generosity. Aversive emotions tend to make us focus inwards, analysing our problems over and over again and trying to find a way through them. If we force ourselves, we can look outward, find someone else with a problem, perhaps, and help them.

Compassion also has a physical manifestation in the heart area. It feels like a gentle warm smile. We have all felt this deep manifestation of love. Not romantic love but an accepting, all-encompassing love. Generally, we have felt it in nature. When we stand on a hilltop and look at a beautiful view, we have felt it. In Buddhism, we call this metta. It is a very enlivening, rejuvenating emotion, warming our entire body and bringing energy into us. We can cultivate this. The practice is called the metta bhavana. Literally, the cultivation of loving kindness.

This is a habit-forming practice. We are seeking to develop a habit of awareness towards the heart. A habit of focusing on the positive and of looking outward to others and to the world.

The Magic of Noticing – Andy Spragg

4.7.3 Delusion

Desire and aversion are fairly obvious roots of suffering. We can quite easily see how we get caught up in constantly craving the good things and pushing away the things we do not like.

So, what of delusion? What is this and how does it cause us suffering? Delusion is a bit of a tricky term to deal with. It sounds very derogatory. To call someone delusional is a bit of an insult! In truth though, until we are enlightened, we are all delusional.

What, then, do we mean by delusion? The mind essentially forms an overlay or a veil over true experience all the time. It does this because embedded within it are mental habits. Religious beliefs, prejudices and our traits established by our parents and by our society. Some have been handed down to us by evolution, through our genetic makeup.

Essentially, we receive information in, about the world, through our five senses, but we are not yet consciously aware of it. The mind then kicks in. It doesn't just "see" the world. It overlays the experience with all those mental habits, biases, expectations etc. The mind essentially sees what it expects to see. The most amazing example of this is where we come upon a stranger. We've never met them before, and they haven't even spoken to us yet. Already we have started to form an opinion of them based on the clothes they wear and the body shape and "look". We might have even decided whether we like them or not. How unfair is that?

None of this is bad or wrong. It is just what the mind does. It is very human. The mind forms its view of the world based on our lives. What we have seen, been told, done.

The Magic of Noticing – Andy Spragg

Don't underestimate the difficulty of working on this area. What plays into this is the very essence of "me" or "I". As soon as we start to work on this, we discover it is our very own characters which are playing in! Some of the concepts that we realise are colouring our view of the world will potentially be very dear to us and to let go of them will require significant work. Maybe the work of a lifetime!

We all tend to one of the three areas of suffering. Our character will be mainly grasping, aversive or delusional. But we can of course move into any of the other areas, depending on our day and what is going on in our life.

For example. You visit your friend in their house. As you walk in, your particular type will be revealed to you.

Desiring - "Wow, look at that fireplace. I would love a fireplace like that"

Aversive -" uhh, I don't like the colours they've chosen"

Delusional -" what am I doing here, I'm not really sure why I've been invited over, what's the motive?"

There are aspects of all three of these in all of us, but we will tend to slide towards one of them.

But we should not despair. There is good that comes out of all three when we take a look at the positive side. The grasping and desiring character tends to bring energy into a situation. They typically uplift the situation and often take the lead. The aversive person spots the pitfalls and risks in a situation, helping us to not dive into a bad situation. The delusional person is really important. It is out of these people that the big ideas often emerge from. They spot the answers to our problems.

What about spirituality? These roots of suffering can even appear here. For example, in meditation. Even here, these three states creep in.

Desiring - "I'd love a zafu (a meditation cushion) like that. With a cushion like that I could truly reach deep meditative states." Aversive – "he's not sitting right. His posture's all wrong, that's not going to take him forward."

Delusion - "here I am meditating on my cushion, my meditation is so deep I can feel the neutrons firing in my brain, I can feel the flow of enlightenment gathering in my body, this is it, I'm on my way, I'm becoming an enlightened being."

Unfortunately, none of these perspectives are going to take us forward. We need to let go of these states.

So, what's the answer? How do we approach this? We meditate. We practise. Meditation itself is about developing the mental habit that we will then take out and apply in our daily lives. It is about developing a habit of mind watching. The answer to this will not come immediately. It will be a gradual progression of noticing in our lives. That's all we have to do. The magic is in the noticing. When we notice desire, aversion or delusion in our lives, their influence over us is weakened. But we have to notice first. Meditation builds a habit of mind watching – noticing.

4.8 Habit, one of our biggest hindrances, can also become one of our greatest allies

Sometimes it is good to take a step back from life and see what is causing you the most difficulty. When we mostly do this, however, we tend to look at the things that are outside of us. We look at the things that cause us difficulty from the perspective of things happening to us. It is very easy to focus on those things that happen to us in this way, essentially laying blame on the things that happen to us. It is easy for example, if we are overweight, to blame the foods we eat, the nature of our work or even, radically, our own bodies, where we subscribe to a common myth perhaps that we have a slow metabolism. Actually, people who are overweight generally have a faster metabolism, as the body is functioning under a level of stress. The heart rate is generally higher, and the rate of breathing is faster.

When we take this approach of looking outside of ourselves, we then start to think about and imagine how we can change these things or remove them from our lives in some way. So, if we are blaming our job, we might try getting a new job. But of course, the thing that has not changed is us. We take ourselves with us to the new job. We then start looking at the new job for satisfaction. Maybe we experience it at first. But after a while the same dissatisfaction creeps in.

As we start to practise mindfulness, we begin to realise that working in this external way rarely gives us the results we are looking for.

The Magic of Noticing – Andy Spragg

In mindfulness we discover that our only other option is to look inside ourselves and understand how we react to the things that happen to us. It is here where we discover the things that cause our suffering and also the things that limit our ability to introduce change in our lives. It is our reaction. It is the mind!

This is not an easy journey. Ingrained habit may have developed over years. But we do have things that can help us on this journey. Techniques we can employ to let go of unwholesome habit and develop the wholesome.

Habit is in every aspect of our lives. It is buried in our physical movement and it is buried in the way we think and the way we react to things. When we first consider habit, we tend to focus on those habits that make the papers, alcohol or drug use, for example. But habit is present in us all the time. Some of it has been generously given to us by our parents or by society itself. Some of it we have cultivated by ourselves. It is not necessarily bad. For example, most of us, when given something, say "thank you". This is a pretty good habit, in my opinion!

Our habits feed our emotions. This is why they are so powerful. If you look at any of the habits that exist in you, you will discover emotion sitting behind to a greater or lesser extent, but there, nonetheless.

Where does habit start? In the mind, of course. What else is there? Even physical habit. If we develop a tight, intense mind that always responds to situations in life with conflict and a tense nature, this will reflect in our bodies. Even our walking gate is habitual.

The Magic of Noticing – Andy Spragg

Habit, of course, sits in memory. But we call the memory that we consider in Buddhist thinking the store-consciousness. Memory isn't just the picture book stuff that we are consciously aware of. It is also sitting in our subconscious. The subconscious store is a great deal larger. We have our religious beliefs in here. Our deep prejudices. And our habit.

So how can we possibly work on this? Well, the truth is, we are always working on our subconscious mind but usually we are not doing this deliberately and we are not aware of it. Every time we react to something in the world, deep habit is triggered in our minds.

Scientists now recognise that in each and every split second, approximately 9000 sensory stimulations touch our five senses. We cannot cope with all of these of course, so we only become consciously aware of nine! But all 9000 touch us. As I explained in section 4.2 they pass through our sense organs and what happens next happens extremely fast. The full power of the mind then kicks in.

Think of this all of this as a farmer's field, and we are the farmer. We are watering and nurturing some of the plants in the field and letting others wither and die. We can either do this with care and attention, choosing which plants to nourish. Or we can just water the field in a haphazard way. If we water haphazardly, the natural dips and troughs in the field will choose where the water runs to and the plants in this area of the field will flourish. If we don't watch our minds, they absolutely behave like this. Those thoughts that get the most nourishment will flourish even more. Lo and behold, the field of the mind has dips and ruts. This is habit! So,

The Magic of Noticing – Andy Spragg

our way to handle this is to notice. To do that, we have to mind watch. This is mindfulness practise. We have to observe our minds at work, noticing where habit is potentially influencing us. Some of this will need a great sense of honesty and a real desire to change. Because some of the things we will be looking into here are probably what we would describe as "me".

There is, however, an easy way and a hard way to this. Usually, when we consider dealing with habit, we think about stopping something. This is the hard way. Giving up smoking for example. For a few habits, this really is the only approach. But for some habits, we are better to add in additional new positive habits, that will gradually replace the old negative ones. We can essentially fill in the dips and ruts in that field. A good friend of mine, a practitioner who teaches nutrition, recommends this approach with diet. Instead of cutting stuff out, start by adding more healthy stuff in. Here, she suggests adding in a new habit of a raw food smoothie every day. Build in this habit, between lunch and dinner, mid-way between. You will find the desire to snack on unhealthy stuff quite naturally subsides.

This approach can be used in many areas where ingrained habit is really leading to poor health; mental health too. If you have a lifestyle where you come home and simply slump on the sofa, eating crisps and drinking while you watch the TV, stopping the crisps and the drink is probably not going to work for you with ease. Pretty quickly you will find yourself reaching back for them again. Instead, you really do need to take a look at your lifestyle and introduce a new habit. You need to find something you enjoy doing and start doing that a couple of times a week in the evening.

Gradually, the old habit of slobbing on the sofa night after night will not carry the same attraction. It's okay once in a while but not every night!

So, in making changes in your life, have a look at your habit. See what you habitually do each day and see how this is affecting your health and well-being. Then, don't think about ripping stuff out. Think about what you could add in! See what you could do that you would enjoy doing and how that could negate the effect of perhaps the less positive habits in your life. Most importantly, don't be hard on, or judgmental towards yourself. That will just leave you feeling miserable (and that in itself may even be habitual).

When we give something up, this is generally associated with quite negative thought processes. This is what makes it so difficult. However, when we add in something new, we can use that emotional engagement with more effect. We can be truly excited about doing something new. Emotional engagement in something new really gets us going. That will carry us through for a while, then we have to call on resolve to keep us moving forward. Any time we take on something new we need this. Resolve is made up of two things - conviction and commitment. Conviction is the belief that we are doing something for good reason. It really is worth doing. Commitment is our personal, heartfelt desire to battle forward and keep going. Working in this way we can truly get ourselves behind making a change in our lives. We can get interested in it, excited about it. We are then using the natural, positive behaviours of our mind as an ally to help us.

The Magic of Noticing – Andy Spragg

So, how do we practically develop our resolve? Again, here we can use the natural function of the mind to help us. Set out your intent right at the start of each and every day to stay with the determination to make your change, whatever it may be. The simple little exercise settles down in to the subconscious. We are sending a message deep into our minds to stay with this. This will sit there in our subconscious right through the day, slowly redeveloping habit. Why not write out a little mantra about your intent. Pop it beside your bed so that you see it each morning. Then, as your feet touch the floor, say your mantra. Remind yourself what you are going to do with this day.

Most of us have important things to do in our lives. But you could argue that one of our most important projects is this very one. To develop ourselves in a way which takes us forward in a healthy and wholesome way, in terms of our physical, mental, social and spiritual health. To look at our deep habits in all these areas and ask ourselves, is this wholesome for me and for the people close to me?

With meditation, which is primarily mental but for those that practise it, we know it has a physical side. We work by noticing the process of our thoughts and how they materialise in emotions and on into actions. In this way we can start to change our character and unravel some of that habit.

This mind watching, itself, needs to come from habit. So that we actually remember to do it. Noticing the mental objects that emerge. This is our teacher. The magic is just in the noticing.

The Magic of Noticing – Andy Spragg

4.9   What of mindfulness?

Mindfulness isn't something we do. It is a mind state that we arrive at.

This might sound tricky to the western mind as we get so used to 'doing'.

The Buddha said that the Dhamma is visible, timeless and calling out to be approached and seen. It is not something mysterious and remote, but is the truth of our own experience. Mindfulness gives us access to that truth. This truth, in order to be liberating, has to be known directly. It cannot be accepted on faith.

Everything we experience and come in to contact with is experienced through awareness. You could say that when we talk about mindfulness, we are really saying awareness. Controversially, Awareness that we spend in most of our time is not very mindful. It is not the true experience. Mind doesn't always present a true picture to us. It doesn't tell us the truth about a situation.

If look at the analogy of the journey. These days we drive around, led by our GPS systems in our cars. How often do these stories come through the media of someone who ends up stuck in a field of cows or stranded in a river because they have blindly followed their GPS? GPS is phenomenal technology, but it isn't always an accurate portrayal of the true nature of the roads.

Our own awareness is very much like this. It does not necessarily tell us the truth because of the way our minds work. Our usual mode of conscious awareness colours the direct experience with embellishments from our own minds. Mental habit, prejudices, deeply held religious beliefs, attitudes, all come in to play. We are usually not consciously aware of this process. We don't see the way the mind overlays everything, we utterly 'believe' the stories it is telling us. Just as we believe and trust our GPS.

Our mind is able to operate in two states.

1.   Being aware. Using the five senses to understand what is happening around us and within us

2.   Creating. (e.g. planning, expecting, imaging, worrying, scheming etc)

When we are in the awareness state, we are completely in the pleasant moment. When we are in the creating state, we are in the future, in the past or somewhere else. We are not in the present moment!

Actually, the trouble starts when we do both of these at once and we don't realise. Our creating ability embellishes what is actually happening, we don't notice this behaviour and we blindly follow it. This is called delusion.

So, mindfulness clears up this cognitive field, seeing the embellishments we are overlaying and letting them go. We cannot just stop the process of the mind and the way it works. That is its job after all. So, we have to start to practice in a way that sees this process going on and looks behind it to see the experience directly.

Think of a field, that a farmer is going to plant his crop in. If he does not remove the weeds and grass first and reveal the topsoil, the crop will not grow well at all. We have to work in this way with mindfulness.

This is why I said at the start, mindfulness is not something that we do. It is a mind state that we end up in. The mind does many things. It judges, plans, criticises, associates and so on. These are all doings. The mindfulness state just watches and notes each moment as it arises and passes away.

In this way, mindfulness facilitates deep concentration or wisdom depending on how we utilise it.

Let's take a look at some formal definition of mindfulness itself. This has now become a secular practice in the western world but here we are going back to the Buddha's original teaching.

The practice of mindfulness is primarily set out in the Satipathanna Sutra. A writing that forms part of the Pali Canon; the Buddhist Bible if you like. This sets out four fields of mindfulness.

1.   Contemplation of the body.

2.   Contemplation of feeling

3.   Contemplation of the state of mind

4.   Contemplation of phenomena

The Body. This is the starting point. It is here that we see the introduction of the breath, but also the body scan. Even at this stage we learn a great deal about just looking with bare attention. Very quickly, if we aren't vigilant, the mind creeps in. It can overlay all sorts of interpretations and embellishments. At this

The Magic of Noticing – Andy Spragg

stage we are looking to just notice when the mind does this and let it go. Come back to the object of our focus and see it directly. Although this is the first of the fields, in many ways it is the most important, and through the mindfulness of breathing the Buddha achieved enlightenment. It can take us all the way through to nirvana if we are diligent in our practice. Out of it comes wisdom; a deep understanding of the nature of all things. When we focus on the body and we see it as it is, we see pure impermanence. There is nothing static. Nothing that lasts. Over time we start to really experience the lack of a permanent self and we let go of ego.

The Feelings. This is where we take things a stage further and notice how our mind makes choices about how we react to things. Desire, aversion or neutrality. This happens exceptionally fast, so we do not often notice the mind embellishing the experience and this therefore informs us of the choice it has made.

The Mind. Here we can simply examine our experience of mind state, examining conscious awareness with interest and noting that even the mind has pleasurable and unpleasurable mental objects that flow through and how we cling to the pleasurable and push away the unpleasurable. Just to start practising at this level takes us a long way into understanding ourselves. Here we are trying to access pure mind. Think of a bottle of water. There are two things here, the bottle itself and the water within it. The water will take the shape of the bottle into which it is poured. It is the same water, but it has a different shape dependent on the bottle. We can view our mind like this. Our mind is the bottle. Depending on our mind shape different thoughts or mental objects will arise.

The Magic of Noticing – Andy Spragg

If our mind is compassionate, then our mental objects will be compassionate in nature.

Phenomena. This is fascinating. I believe there is a simple way to view this, and it presents to us a potential for a deep understanding into the nature of our life. We can see and experience that the only reason the universe knows it exists is because of minds being present in the universe. Sentient beings can be seen as bubbles of awareness appearing in the vastness of the universe and allowing it to see itself. So, given what we know about how our own minds alter our perceptions we now start to take a fresh look at the universe and realise that the world we see is our world, presented on the mirror of our own minds. Anyone who meditates for a while starts to discover how our minds do not tell us the truth, so the world is not really like our perception of it. The distortion can be very subtle. For example, we may misinterpret a friend's comment and read an incorrect view into our friend, whereupon they become an enemy! Or we may view a whole country as an enemy because of what we have read in the newspapers.

The Magic of Noticing – Andy Spragg

Chapter 5. Meditation

We have looked at the basics of Buddhist practice and now we know why we suffer. But how do we change things? We have mentioned mindfulness a few times, but how do we develop mindfulness? How do we introduce this into our daily lives? Meditation is the answer.

In this section I am setting out the main approaches to meditation. There are four key meditation practices that we can use to experience and study all of the thoughts and approaches described in this book.

My recommendation to you is to familiarise yourself with these practices by doing them. Become familiar with the basic practices presented here, then later in the book I will refer back to them and recommend how you can 'tweak' the practice to examine a particular area of study.

You can find recordings of the led meditations on our web site – https://www.thesanghahouse.co.uk/meditations

But, before we dive into the practices themselves, let's take a look at the things that stop us making progress in meditation – The Hindrances, as they are known in Buddhism.

5.1   The hindrances to meditation

In meditation, we understand that to make progress, we must move beyond/let go of the hindrances to meditation. The Buddha set out these main hindrances. They are desire for sense pleasures,

The Magic of Noticing – Andy Spragg

aversion and ill will, sloth, torpor, dullness, boredom, restlessness and worry, and doubt or stubborn scepticism.

In working with these hindrances and applying mindfulness to our experiences of them, we discover that they can become sources for meditation themselves!

In handling the hindrances, the Buddha advised us to take the hindrance through five steps:

- recognise the presence of the hindrance.
- noticing when a hindrance is absent
- learning what causes the hindrance to arise
- understand what can cause the hindrance to cease
- investigate how to avoid the hindrance re-arising

Each of us will have one or two hindrances that primarily arise in our meditation. Provided we can stay present and mindful, we can follow through these five steps. But we do this in a way that is experiential, rather than trying to figure our way through them with academic thinking.

Let us take an example, restlessness and worry. For me, this has been a constant working area for my meditation. It arises in me in the form of planning. When a worry arises, I straight away start to plan my way around it and try to fix it. By working on the body scan, we notice deeply how worry affects the body. We notice the quickening of the heart, the effect on the breath and the increase in energy in the body. When we feel this, we understand the deep correlation between the mind and the body. In this way, we focus on the body again. Quite naturally, this distracts our mind away from the worry itself and we begin to notice the body settle and

The Magic of Noticing – Andy Spragg

become still again. As we become settled and still, we see that this is due to the absence of the worrying thought. Of course, this tends to work in cycles. The moment we notice that the body has settled, and we notice that it is due to the absence of the worrying though, the thought re-appears! But this in itself teaches us a great deal, because we really start to see how the worry, (the hindrance), is affecting us. So, we may well have to go around this cycle a good number of times. Gradually, we learn to notice the very subtle arising of the hindrance and drive our attention to the body. This is in itself, the fifth step. We have taught ourselves how to stop it arising again.

5.2   How do we sit?

I know it sounds a strange question, but it is a very important place to start. Firstly, you must be comfortable. Many people coming to meditation think that they have to sit cross-legged on the floor, and they expect to be uncomfortable and have to work through this. Not at all. It is important that we are well supported, self-supported, gently upright. But definitely not uncomfortable. So, by self-supported, I suggest that you sit in a way that the spine can gently support itself. If we lean back in a chair, in a slouched, relaxed position, we are likely to fall asleep. So, bring yourself forward on the chair and arrange your upper body so it balanced and upright over the sitting bones.

You can sit cross legged on the floor if you have the flexibility in your body or you can invest in a meditation stool. These are very good if you wish to connect with the ground more fully. You sit in a kneeling position. But a chair is just fine!

5.3   The Body Scan

I always start my personal meditation with the body scan. It helps us to settle into the posture and arrive in the moment. However, the body scan itself can be a very effective meditation and personally I have made some of my most effective progress using it. It can teach us a great deal.

The body scan is a very powerful tool for insight meditation, seeing deeply into the nature of things. As we drop into the body, looking deeply, we see things that were in front of us all the time, but we hadn't noticed.

I also teach Tai Chi and I always encourage an understanding that the mind leads the body. The mind moves first, and the body follows. This has not come from my exploration of tai chi, but from my meditation. It reveals to us at a very deep level, that the mind and body are one. In our work with this meditation, we tune in closer and closer to the correlation between the mental objects that arise in the mind and their effect on the body and the subtle changes we experience.

Nowhere is this apparent more than when we explore our stomach and heart area. Here we have the seat of our emotions. Our emotions are triggered by the mental objects that flow through the mind. We see very clearly how the emotions are not the thoughts. Thoughts trigger the emotions and then feed and justify them. The emotions themselves are physical sensations that are going on right through the body. It is these we focus on. We don't even try to label the emotion. We just experience it deeply, studying the physical feeling. No labelling, just feeling. In this way, even our most negative emotions can become a meditation subject and we can take a deep interest in it. Our meditation helps us to deeply feel our emotions but inhibits the amount of control they have over us.

Meditation utilises two main types of concentration. The single pointed type, to the exclusion of everything else. Or alternatively, a more expansive concentration where everything is experienced. A bird singing, the honk of a car horn, the pain in your knee, a thought flowing through the mind. The body scan meditation utilises both of these approaches. We home in on individual sensations in an area of the body but we also have an expansive awareness. Building up a picture of the whole body and even of the space in which it is sitting. This is very important. It can lead to an understanding of the difference between duality and non-duality. In other words, our usual perception of life is that there is a "me" and there is everything outside of me that might cause me harm and gives me a target to blame perhaps for my misfortune. This is a position of duality. Non-duality takes that away. We perceive no separation between us and the world. Instead, there is Deep connection. Actually, this is staring us in the face. What happens out there in the world has a direct effect on our bodies. An experience of the world around us cuts deeply into our very centre. Our heart. Likewise, we reflect the nature of our thoughts on the world around us and perform actions. So, there is no duality. We are inextricably linked to the world around us. The boundary between us and the world is not really there. The more we practise with the body scan, this apparently simple approach to meditation, the more these understandings reveal themselves to us.

The Magic of Noticing – Andy Spragg

Probably the two deepest understandings that comes to us, with regular practice of the body scan, are the lack of permanence in us and the letting go of the notion of a "self". The more we look directly into the nature of our existence and the more we explore that directly, the less we can find about our experience that is permanent. It is worth keeping this in mind when you practise. Go in and look for anything that is permanent about your experience. Can you find anything to grab on to?

5.3.1 The Body Scan – step by step

- Settle yourself down in a comfortable seated posture and let your eyes close.
- Tune in to the space around you and feel yourself settling in. Aware of your body sitting in your space. Stay away from thought.
- Take a couple of deep, relaxing breaths.
- Now we work through the body. Start down in the feet and gradually work up through the body. Take your awareness into the body and feel the sensations there as you travel through. Notice when thought arises and let it go and come back to the body and pure awareness of sensations. Expectation may come up, let that go. Visualization may emerge, let that go too.
- Don't forget the heart area and gut. Here, notice how the area feels. This is where the energy of your emotions lives. Again, always stay away from thought. Emotions are very strong prompts for thoughts, so we have to work hard to concentrate on pure awareness of the sensations.
- Once we have worked right through the body, we can bring our experience of all these sensations together and sit

in pure awareness. Our body, our emotions, the space around us.

5.4   Meditation on the breath

In Buddhist practice this is known as anapanasati. It is the meditation the Buddha was using when he gained enlightenment. Simple to describe, far from easy to do. What makes it difficult is the mind's tendency to wander. When we use this meditation, we are simply watching the breath and its sensations. The sensations of the breath, seeking to keep our awareness gently fixed onto the sensation. However, the mind intrudes and pulls us away. This is why the meditation is instrumental in our change. It requires the development of concentration and it requires us to develop an ability to notice when the mind has wandered. Just by noticing, we start to see what the mind is doing. We start to learn to draw back from thoughts. To become mindful of our own mind and our own stream of consciousness. This "watching" in itself becomes habitual. We are developing a habit of mind watching.

Start by sitting in a comfortable posture. You can use the body scan meditation first to bring a sense of gentle and general awareness to yourself, your body and your space. Even this early on in the meditation the mind may interfere with thoughts so notice if this happens and draw gently back to your experience.

Now gently start to draw attention to the sensation of the breath. I suggest starting in the chest area. You can feel the chest rise and fall with the breathing. Often, when we become aware of the breath, we start to influence it. To slow it or deepen it. This is the mind interfering again with expectation and control. Let that go.

Just allow the breath to be as fast or slow as it wants. This is itself a learning. To see how the mind plays in and interferes.

Then, become aware of the full path of the breath. Feeling the breath enter the nostrils, move down the back of the throat, through the chest area and coil in the belly. Then uncoil and travel back out. Just gentle awareness to the full path of the breath.

To help deepen the concentration and ability to keep the mind gently engaged on the breath we can use a word. Words can be very powerful in meditation. For example, I use "calm" a great deal in my meditation to settle my awareness and concentration. As you gently breathe in and out, while watching the body and the sensations of the breath, hear the word "calm" echo in the mind on each out-breath. Let it have its effect on mind and body. Breath by breath, feeling yourself becoming calmer, more settled, more still.

To go deeper, you can become aware of the thousands of sensations that you felt throughout the body, in the body scan and experience how the breathing process affects these. Feeling the whole body breathing.

Ensure you stay with searching for direct experience. Do not start expecting things or visualising things. Remember, meditation is also about examining the roots of our suffering. One of these is delusion; the mind overlaying and distorting our true experience.

5.5   Just sitting

At some point, we must learn to accept the nature of mind; its chaotic nature and the way it is. Just sitting is a very effective

The Magic of Noticing – Andy Spragg

meditation for this. Here, rather than having a focus, we simply sit with awareness of anything that arises in our experience.

I suggest starting with a body scan to become aware of all the thousands of sensory experiences in the body. Then, widen out to your space around you - sounds, smells etc, working with your five senses. Then also become aware of Mind. The nature of Mind and the mental objects flowing through it. But it is most important not to get drawn in by the stories within the thoughts. Just notice the thoughts arise and let them go. When we notice a thought from the outside, so to speak, we find that the thought loses its power and fades away. The magic is in the noticing.

5.6   Metta bhavana

The Metta Bhavana meditation is exceptionally important. Its translation is literally the Cultivation Of (Bhavana) Metta (Loving Kindness). For a detailed description of compassion take a look at section 6.3, but here I am going to take you through the metta bhavana practice. Here, we are looking at heart emotion. Like all Buddhist meditations, this one is also experiential. We are looking for a genuine feeling in the heart space. It feels like a soft warm smile. It may "feel" as if it has colour associated with it. A warm yellow perhaps. But don't get too hung up with trying to see colours. I have always found that it is more beneficial to look for actual physical sensation. As we practise, we learn to feel a great deal in our heart space.

5.6.1   Compassion towards self

In many religions, we read that in order to love others we must learn to love oneself. Why is this? Because, simply put, if we love ourselves our heart and our experience will be relaxed and open rather than closed off. We will be able to connect much more deeply in our experience of others if we are in that open-hearted place.

So, we start here. As always, I recommend you start with a body scan meditation first, to bring your awareness thoroughly into the present moment. Then, start to shift your awareness to self. See your body, see your mind, see all its complexity. Everything we love in life has three main things in common. These things we love generally have a complexity about them. They have a feeling of vulnerability and they are impermanent. When we look deeply into ourselves, we see these aspects about us. We must look as if seeing from outside of ourselves without judgement. We notice if resistance or tension comes up in our experience. This can be due to all sorts of emotions triggered by our past. I must emphasise, this meditation is not about digging into these areas to understand them or even figure out when they occurred. We are here to simply work on compassion. So, relax and soften into those feelings of resistance or tension, particularly in the heart area. When tension and resistance are softened in this way, the heart is receptive and open. Traditionally we offer ourselves a simple phrase – "May I be healthy, happy and free from suffering". Say this to yourself, again noticing if there is any resistance or tension to it and soften.

5.6.2 Compassion to the good friend

The meditation now gets easier at this point. We bring to mind a good friend. When we do this, metta (compassion and friendship) are experienced. That warm smile in the heart area. See your friend's face in your mind, their smile. Hear them say your name

The Magic of Noticing – Andy Spragg

and you say theirs. You can replay an episode of time you spent together but remember that we are here to be fully present and aware of compassion itself so try not to get lost in reverie. Humans are complex creatures with even more complex relationships. Other emotions may arise. If they do, do not try to understand them. Allow them to arise and then focus again on that feeling of metta in your heart as you contemplate your friend. We can also recognise the complexity of this friends life, their vulnerability in it and the challenge that this gives them, just as it does us. As we know them well, this allows us to really empathise with their position. We can offer them the traditional phrase in our minds. "May you be healthy, happy and free from suffering. "

5.6.3   Compassion to the neutral person

We bring to mind someone who we know but not well. So, we cannot have developed any strong feelings one way or the other. We may know their name, or we may not. We might know them from the job they do. The corner shopkeeper, the postman etc.

As we consider them, perhaps visualising them at their place of work, we bring a sense of soft awareness to the heart space again. Offering this out to them. Again, we can perhaps see and understand that they also have great complexity in life and a naturally vulnerable nature. We bring empathy into the picture again. Wish them well – "May you be healthy, happy and free from suffering"

5.6.4   Compassion to the challenge

Then, we come to what is probably the hardest part of all. The challenge. The person who has perhaps wronged us in some way. Maybe they refused to do as we asked and they make our blood boil. Or worse, they stole from us. Again, it does need to be someone you know. This is the hardest part of the meditation. As you bring them to mind, notice the nature of your reaction. Feel the tension arise in the body and emotion emerge. Most important, stay away from justification or judgement. Don't try to solve the problem or understand anything. What you are looking here is pure experience. You are looking to see the tension and difficult emotion as just another experience to observe. Then, soften into the experience. Opening in the heart space. Remember, you are not lessening your position in relation to this other person, they aren't even here and they are unaware that you are doing this meditation. This is purely about your practice. So soften in the heart space and offer out that warm smile of metta. Understand their complexity in their life and their vulnerability. But again, not with judgement and not with conceit. Offer them the message with a genuine heart felt wish – "May you be healthy, happy and free from suffering"

5.6.5   Widening out

We can now take our awareness wider. Seeing our friends and family in our mind. The whole town and perhaps the whole world.

The Metta Bhavana is a very difficult meditation. But stick at it, it can be transformational. Starting to make you truly see how even in difficulty we can remain mindful, aware, grounded and compassionate.

Chapter 6. Exploring Buddhist thinking

The first chapter has explored a basic understanding of Buddhist thinking and set out the main approaches to meditation.

In this chapter, I will take you into some of the deeper aspects of Buddhist thinking and explore how we can use this to further loosen the chains of our own minds and its influence on our life. Also introducing some of my own thoughts and discoveries along the way.

6.1   Finding daily opportunities for meditation and practice

The more we practise, the more we find opportunity for practice. Remember that meditation is developing new mental habit. But we cannot develop habit unless we actually practise. One of the biggest comments I hear from the people I teach is that they are so busy they cannot find time to meditate. This is not true. The more we meditate, the more time we find we have. But we can also find little pockets of time during our day. These opportunities may only be a few seconds long, but they all still count towards building that all-important habit.

We truly have a constant supply of experiences that we can draw on. Here we examine a few mind states that we all experience, how they at first feel detrimental and how we can start to see them as opportunities.

Mindfulness is of course challenging us to exist fully and completely in the present moment, noticing things exactly as they are. What is it that takes us away from this? Well, in our modern world there are many things but two of the most common mental states are waiting and rushing.

6.1.1   Waiting and rushing

Mindfulness is of course challenging us to exist fully and completely in the present moment, noticing things exactly as they are. What is it that takes us away from this? Well, in our modern world there are many things but two of the main mental activities are waiting and rushing.

Think about where your mind is, when you are engaged in either of these.

These two are rather contradictory when you think about it. Waiting leaves us feeling rather static, as if we are stalled and can't move on until whatever it is that we are waiting for, arrives. Rushing has a sense of movement about it. We aren't going to be in a satisfactory, contented state until we get somewhere or complete something.

If we look at waiting first. Just spend a day noticing how much you tend to spend waiting. Even seemingly inconsequential things we wait for. A lot of what we wait for isn't actually going to create long term contentment. It is satisfying a very short-term desire. How long do we spend waiting for the kettle to boil? How long do we spend waiting for our PC's to wake up? Call backs, emails etc. So much time spent waiting.

But we can be a great deal more subtle than this if we really apply mindfulness and pay attention, we start to notice how the mind works. How we are working on a particular mental problem. Searching for a solution perhaps. Lo and behold, hidden in there, we find waiting. We find ourselves waiting for the right mental answers to appear in our minds. Waiting for our thoughts to give us the answers, or solving a problem perhaps. However, if we pay attention and become mindful, we find that the mind does not work like that. Answers are not presented to us because we have waited for the mind to finish its processing. Instead, answers are presented to us out the beautiful chaos of the mind; almost being served up out of nowhere. So why are we waiting? If we just get on with life, the mind will continue its creative process anyway. Also, of course, when we are waiting, the mind is thinking about the thing we are waiting for. The mind is not present. It is painting a picture of a future time when the thing we are waiting for has arrived.

Remember what it was like when we were kids waiting for Christmas? We would paint a picture in our minds of life with all those lovely presents we had put on our Christmas list. How painfully exciting that felt!

A lot of waiting carries with it strong emotion. Anxiety and worry are generally exaggerated by the waiting process. What are we doing when we wait for something that is carrying with it worry or anxiety? The mind, of course, is firing up and concentrating on the perceived problem. Generally, it is rolling the story behind the problem around and around, trying to find a way out of the worry and anxiety and find a solution perhaps. The story is replayed over and over again.

Of course, when we do this, the mind then further encourages the emotion to develop and the worry and anxiety deepens. Potentially, if this continues it can lead to real suffering.

The Magic of Noticing – Andy Spragg

If we can develop a habit of mindfulness, then waiting presents us with an opportunity for practice. If there is truly nothing else to do while we wait, then why not meditate? Then, because the mind is just being in the present moment, it is no longer painting that picture of life when the waited for event arrives. It is merely being present. Magically, we are then no longer waiting!

So, to practise with waiting, we must first start to observe what happens when we are waiting. What we are waiting for and what the mind feels like in that waiting state. What mental objects are flowing through and what emotions are being triggered. Lo and behold, if we do this, we are no longer waiting. We are now doing something useful. The waiting itself has become a meditation subject and we can study with interest.

What of rushing? The two are related sometimes. We rush because we think the thing we are waiting for will happen faster if we rush. So here again, we are rushing because we believe we will get to a contented place quicker. We can look at the things we are rushing for and ask ourselves if they will leave us with long term contentment? There are times where we must move fast. If we are in a profession where some degree of speed is needed, then clearly, we have to apply it. A surgeon saving a patient's life sometimes must apply speed to make sure they don't lose the patient. A racing driver would not be particularly good at their job if they didn't have an element of "rushing" about themselves! But we won't need to do this all the time. We need to take care that our life doesn't disappear for us because we rush right through it. Rushing can be all consuming. When we are rushing, we can literally lose our minds! It's an interesting expression "lose our

The Magic of Noticing – Andy Spragg

minds". For me this implies that we lose every little bit of self-awareness. The mind is totally and utterly caught up in the thing we are rushing for. We are not even aware of the rushing!

We use our mindfulness practice; noticing when we are rushing, what happens when the desire to rush arises and to take a look at our emotional relationship with the thing we are rushing for. To truly ask the question, why are we rushing and what are we rushing for? That old question of "is this wholesome?" Is also a good one to ask. Listen to the dialogue in the mind. We will often hear ourselves arguing the case for our rushing. Are those arguments actually true? Is there really a need to rush?

Again, when we work in this way, we are bringing the mind back to the present. We aren't thinking about the thing we are rushing for. We are being fully present as we examine the nature of rushing. And again, the rushing immediately dissolves. By definition, because we are aware of the rushing in the mind, we are aware, therefore fully present through the awareness and no longer rushing!

We also tend to find then that the clearer we think, as a result of letting the mind rest and open, the more we see that the reasons for the rushing were artificial.

So, we can bring both of these practices squarely into our meditation to develop a practice of mind watching, relating to these two areas. During meditation both of these mind states can arise. We can be waiting for something to happen or we can find a desire for the meditation to progress quickly to some form of conclusion, perhaps to a previous blissful state that we have

The Magic of Noticing – Andy Spragg

experienced. We want to drive forward our meditation to achieve that state. Then we find that we are not truly paying attention to the moment. Our meditation has become all about achieving something, and we are either waiting for that or pushing ourselves to achieve it. When we see this, we recognise the state in ourselves and we can simply relax and come fully present again.

The Body Scan meditation (see 5.3) is perfect for investigating this process in the mind. As we travel gently through the body, staying aware of what the mind is doing, we will identify lots of times where the mind is looking for something more interesting, expecting sensations to arise and even wanting to rush ahead to other parts of the body.

Settle into your meditation posture. Don't rush it! Then scan through the body, looking for genuine experience and sensations. Work through from the feet to the top of the head. As you gently travel, keep a watch on whether these two mental states of waiting and rushing arise.

6.1.2   Judging and judgement

This is another area where we have a real opportunity to start to notice our mental process and introduce transformation and change.

We make judgements every day. Judgement is after all, the ability to make a considered opinion. But is carried with it other connotations and we should take a look at them all.

So, probably the most aggressive one is the idea of divine retribution. Here, the understanding is that as we have performed some reprehensible act, that God or the Universe will enforce some form of penalty on us. I am sure that theologians discuss this one for hours. With polarised views looking at a benign and compassionate God could ever pack someone off to Hell for what they have done. Or, from the perspective of the old Vedic view of karma, that everyone involved in the Tsunami in the Far East some years back, somehow deserved it. These ideas just don't quite ring true. Our pure spiritual practice needs to go into this and ask these questions. If these views do not make sense, then I think we can safely say that they are not applicable to us. They rest with superstition (a mental aberration introduced by Mind. Watch out for that one in your practice). But we still need to explore if there is something here. Is there judgement from a universal perspective?

When we meditate on this, we have to look at where the mind and all its superstitious ability is kicking in and try to see past that veil. There is lots of cosmology in Tibetan Buddhism with its many layers. It carries with it the ability to transcend to the upper layers with our spiritual practice each time we go through a rebirth. Interestingly, the realm of the human is seen as a better realm to be in than the realm of the Gods. The Gods have a wonderful life with everything they need. But they don't have suffering. It is this that stops them from achieving enlightenment. Humans have the opportunity to understand and experience suffering. This teaches us much and helps us move towards true enlightenment. I personally find it hard to believe in These realms, but I do find the model it depicts can be found in our own everyday lives. There is the realm of the hungry ghosts. Greed and grasping are a major part of this person's life. They can never satisfy their desire to have more. And there are many Gods. People who have everything.

The Magic of Noticing – Andy Spragg

Decent, moral and ethical people but completely out of touch with the rest of the world. Either way, there is lots of potential for judging here. When someone is not in our realm, there is the potential for judging them.

The next area is where judging is the decision of the court or a judge. I am no expert in the legal system so please forgive my lack of knowledge here. But I do believe in the court system and the need for it. There is a need for judgement here. In the UK we have the jury system, which is ancient and fascinating. Legal scholars can tell you its full history. But to me it does seem to me quite a compassionate approach. Rather than asking a single person to cast the judgement, when that person will bring in their own veil of preconceptions and mental habit, we spread it across 12 people who, because of the complexity of we humans, will have many different perspectives.

Now we move up a layer, to the area of having opinions or making conclusions. These are also judgements. We of course make many hundreds of these every day about pretty much everything. Of course we must. But this area can also result in our disconnection with the world. Where I believe this is most damaging is with people. We form opinions of them even before we know them. They walk up to us in the street and we start to decide things about them. We might even decide if we like them and they haven't even spoken to us yet! Our mindfulness practice here is just to notice the mind doing this; to notice this process going on and, in noticing, we stop and open up to the person in front of us. Of course, people sometimes show their "true colours" to us. But here we need to apply empathy; to stand beside them and see things from their perspective before we judge.

Social media is a riot of judgement. Pick any of the big topics around today that are represented on social media. For example, Covid-19 and our political leaders' ability to lead us through it. A very good example. Take a look at the polarised views expressed in social media and then take a look at the rather personal comments made between people and about people. These are made by people who do not know each other at all, but they form a judgement based on a few lines. And they, I have no doubt, make a whole bunch of assumptions about the other person. In their own mind they are personally claiming to "know" the other person. Social media is just dreadful for this.

Finally, judging is about making informed decisions. For me, I come back to that one question again that I can ask myself. Is this wholesome? Of course, we make lots of mundane decisions each day. It would be rather tiresome if we looked at each and every one and questioned its wholesomeness. But the big questions, those that may carry a spiritual or moral side to them, we should ask, is this wholesome? There will be many, every day.

So, what about meditation? How are we going to bring this into our meditation practice? Clearly, we are doing something very odd if meditation results in a court case!

I think there are two things we need to focus on here - our internal judging and the development of habit to ensure we notice our judging when we are off the cushion.

The Magic of Noticing – Andy Spragg

When we meditate, lots of judging goes on. When the mind wanders, we scold ourselves for not having a concentrated mind. Doubts creep in. "I'll never be able to do this". We judge ourselves. This is all very natural and very human. We bring a sense of gentle nurturing care into the situation, seeing this judging behaviour with good humour, accepting it and letting it go. This forms mental habit.

Keep a sharp eye for self-recrimination and self-blame. When the mind wanders, be gentle on yourself. Bring yourself back to the meditation subject. Perhaps notice the arising of that judging, blaming mind, again with a sense of interest and humour. All of this builds habit in the mind.

Habit, once built, cuts in whenever it feels it belongs. So, this means that this habit that we have built on the cushion, will emerge in our daily life. We will start to see this judging and blaming behaviour in our daily lives.

We use our meditation on the breath (See 5.4) to see when the mind gets judgmental. It may arise as critique. We hear the dialogue of the mind telling us that we are not breathing deeply and slowly enough. When we notice this, we let it go and come back to the breath exactly as it is.

Start with a gentle sit and awareness of the body and your surroundings. Here, you can notice whether waiting and rushing are arising. Then, become aware of the sensation of the breath moving through the body. Keeping yourself focussed on it, see if any feelings of judgement, towards yourself, about the quality of your meditation, or your approach, come up. When they do, smile

The Magic of Noticing – Andy Spragg

at the way the mind works and gently let go and come back to the breath.

6.2   Vedanas

In Chapter 4.2 I presented you with a picture of the senses and explained, from a Buddhist psychology perspective how a sense experience enters the sense organ, then touches Mind for the first time with the sense doors, goes through a selection process – like, dislike or neutral - and then gets embellished by Mind. But there is much more going on! In that selection process, like, dislike or neutral, there a massive process happening, and it all happens, remarkably, in a split second.

The Vedanas are the first response to a sensory stimulation. Usually they are unconscious. i.e. we are not aware that they are happening. But if we pay attention, we will find that we can train ourselves to become aware and notice the process going on. What is it that decides whether something is liked, disliked or frankly rather boring? Marmite™. Here's a good example. We either love it or hate it. But we don't all feel the same about it? Why not? Marmite™ is a good and very simple example, but most things are rather more complex. Our judgement is made based on the contents of our minds. Remember the three parts of the mind? Chapter 4.4, The Manas (the thinking bit), the store consciousness (Memory or mind-store) and the Gardener which can watch these first two working on and interacting with each other. Sitting in our memory or mind-store is a whole host of information which we use in that very instant to decide our choice. So, our deep-seated fears sit here, our religious beliefs, our habits, our desires and our prejudices. They all sit in here and they immediately contribute to our choice of how we feel about the sensory experience. Some of these are exceptionally powerful and they have been embedded into us during our lives. Also, they are not necessarily positive. The most compulsive behaviours in people come out of Vedanas. A lot of our anxiety (even leading to depression if left unchecked) starts from the Vedanas.

The best way to explain how this all works is for me to give you an example. A fictitious example, but one that rings true for many people who have gone through our school systems. Vedanas are especially powerful where a situation of stress occurs in our lives. Essentially, when we experienced stress, trauma, anxiety or even positive emotion such as joy, rapture and excitement, Vedanas get embedded. They are embedded in our very bodies. Remember that the body is as much a part of the store consciousness as mind! Associated at that moment with this "writing" in the body are the sense experiences that were going on at that moment.

6.2.1   The Vedanas - an example

At the age of seven a child at primary school is standing in the playground with the other children. It is a warm summer's day and this child suffers with hay-fever. It makes him wheezy and his eyes sting. The other children do not understand it as they don't suffer with hay-fever. It is sports day coming up and the children are being selected into the teams. This poor boy is never keen on sports and never very practiced because most of the sports practice happens in the summer when the weather is nice, outside in the pollen rich playing fields. The teacher picks the boy for one of the teams. The red team. The team-mates who have already been selected let out an audible groan (kids can be horrible) and unfortunately the teacher does not correct their behaviour.

There is a great deal going on in this picture and a lot of this experience could now become embedded. The child will feel very powerful emotions which result in tension in the heart and the gut. This is establishing the Vedanas. This is how the Vedanas get embedded in us. Strong sensory experience gets associated with strong emotional response and this gets, essentially, recorded in the body. From this point forward, associations will be made with the sense experiences that were happening at the time. The warm summer's day, the smells, figures in authority, the colour red. The Vedanas are established instantaneously so certain sense experiences will be more prevalent and create a strong trigger for the Vedanas.

Of course, we cannot protect ourselves or our children from this kind of experience. This is just part of life. Tough things happen. But as individuals we can start to recognise the Vedanas in ourselves and do something about them. In the case of the little boy, let us say the colour red and authority figures are embedded. In the future, in situations where one or both of these arise in the child's life, there will be a tightening in the boy's heart and gut. This will be unconscious, but it will happen, and it will influence the way the boy acts in the situation, causing a potential for fear or anger which then result in action. If unnoticed, the Vedanas can then get even more deeply ingrained as this may result in further and more extreme emotional misfortune which again results in further stress, tension and tightening in the heart. This may be slight and gentle, but it does deepen. Each episode deepens the

The Magic of Noticing – Andy Spragg

experience. In the worst case the man who grows out of the boy develops a compulsive mistrust of authority figures and ends up with a compulsive disorder associated with the colour red which influences the rest of his life. A very tough mental process is now established here, and it will be a hard one to break.

Not all Vedanas are bad. For me, a certain tick of a clock produces a lovely feeling of safety and calm. This comes from my childhood when I slept in a room in my grandmother's house. My grandparents were wonderful, and I always felt very safe and secure with them.

So how do we deal with the Vedanas? Firstly, we shouldn't see them as bad or evil. This is another thing in our makeup that evolution has had a hand in building. So, the way to approach them is to see their influence as an interesting thing to study in our lives. As I always say, and reflected in the title of this book, the magic is in the noticing. This is all we have to do. We notice how sense objects produce an instantaneous tightening in our heart and gut. Some of these will be surprising and we may not even remember the reason behind them. In our example, the older man may have absolutely no recollection why he has a pathological fear of the colour red. But we notice and we focus on the physical sensation and we mentally soften into it. We apply a gentleness of spirit to it, easing out the tension and replacing it with calmness. We can breathe into it. Developing a habit of paying attention all the time, we notice this tightening arise. Have you ever had a feeling that something awful has happened? It manifests as a superstitious dread that someone close has suffered in some way. Chances are that this is the vedanas at play. A sense trigger that is

The Magic of Noticing – Andy Spragg

buried deep has triggered the physical tightening. There is no need to notice or know the history of the triggered sense itself (although if we can it does help). All we need to do is notice the physical tightening and learn to relax this.

6.2.1.1   *Meditation, vedanas - body scan and the gut*

Because working with the vedanas is all about listening to our body and the way the tension creeps in when they are experienced, we practise using the body scan (See chapter 5.3) and particularly focus on the heart and the gut as it is here that the vedanas produce their affect.

Settle into your meditation posture. Don't rush it!   Then scan through the body, looking for genuine experience and sensations. Work through from the feet to the top of the head. Once you have drawn a complete picture, bring your focus back to the heart and the gut and just practise observing, relaxing and letting go in this area.

6.3   The practice of compassion

Of course, the other key aspect that people understand with Buddhist thinking is the practice of compassion. It is an interesting area to teach and provokes some very interesting reactions! I have had people become extremely defensive when I've suggested teaching them about compassion. Some have responded saying that they didn't like the implication that they weren't compassionate already.

However, this is certainly not the way to look at this. Compassion, within humans, is literally infinite. When we rise in the morning, we can choose that from that point forward we are going to strive to be even more compassionate. So, compassion is certainly not a binary thing (On or Off). We can develop. This is what the Buddhist practice of compassion called Metta Bhavana is all about.

What is it that cause most people suffering in this modern world? I cannot quote firm statistics; only my perceptions, from what I have seen and experienced. And it seems to be separation. Many of us isolate ourselves these days, through fear, primarily and also confusion and delusion.

This isolation is awful. It is almost as if we build our own cell and lock ourselves inside of it.

E.M. Forster wrote "only connect" in Howard's End. Look it up if you have time. It is an interesting quote when taking in the context of the time it was written. For me, this phrase plays a great part in my Buddhist practice and is the antidote to isolation. To break down the walls of our cell, all we have to do is set out each day with the intention to connect. To connect with the people and the world around us.

How do we break down of these walls, from a Buddhist practise perspective? Here, I would like to introduce this word metta. This is a key word in Buddhist practice. The two cornerstones of Buddhist practice are satipathana, which we translate as mindfulness, and metta, which we translate as loving kindness or compassion.

Metta, roughly translated, is loving kindness. These words that are used in Buddhism, satipathana, metta, anapanasati etc. These are all terms expressed in the ancient Indian language of Pali. Pali emerged around the same time as Sanskrit but whereas Sanskrit was a written language and generally only understood by the nobility and senior priests at the time, Pali was the language of the general population. It is an extremely rich language and many of the words need a whole book to translate them. Metta is one such word.

6.3.1   What is metta and how do we practise with it?

Metta is made up of four elements: love, compassion, sympathetic joy and equanimity.

Metta practice and mindfulness practice are not considered separate. They intertwine and support each other. We cannot begin to truly connect unless we can reside fully in the moment. And without a sense of compassion it is almost impossible to let go of our own desires and aversions which colour our view so that we can be completely mindful. I think that metta practice is particularly challenging because of the amount of self-honesty required. As you will see in this section, we can literally fool ourselves that we are going through life with an approach of loving kindness. This is called the close enemy of metta. We appear, to others and to ourselves, to be embracing loving kindness. True self honesty pays attention to the very thoughts that are appearing in our minds, at the moment those thoughts are first born. In Buddhist practice, it really doesn't matter what others think. It is our own internal pure, honest practice that matters. This practice requires us to notice these thoughts and ask ourselves "Is this metta?" This is where the challenge starts and why mindfulness is key.

It is important to understand that the practice is not an intellectual exercise. We have to truly taste the nature of mindfulness and metta and the only way that I have personally found is through meditation. If we try to adopt the practice in our daily, busy lives, we are not giving our mind the opportunity to focus fully and completely on what is arising. We will not see clearly how we are reacting emotionally and consciously to the world and to the people we are coming into contact with. The day will just get in the way.

So, to the four elements of Metta:

6.3.2   Love

The first element of Metta. This is probably the trickiest one of all. The love we are talking about here isn't the one we see portrayed in so many of the movies. It isn't romantic love. It is an unconditional love and it applies to everything we encounter. Ourselves, the world around us, other people. All other people. When you consider that word unconditional, it carries huge implications. Most of the things we consider that we love, come with conditions. Even family members, if they behave badly towards us, we can drop them off our Christmas card list! However, there is no doubt that we have all felt this unconditional love. Any time you have sat on a hilltop and admired the view or the sunset or a gorgeous rainbow, you have felt unconditional love – metta. These things, we don't attach conditions to. We know they are temporary, and we just love these experiences exactly as they are. Through practice, we strive to develop the same kind of love towards all that we find around us. Not easy, but possible.

So, if we then consider the types of things that generally we feel drawn to. In general, these things that we love are usually highly complex and also generally have a feeling of impermanence about them. We might find many things attractive; a rose for example - complex and very vulnerable.

6.3.3 Compassion

The second element of metta. An interesting word. Literally "with passion". Now what does that mean? Well, again, we are not talking here about the type of passion associated with romantic love. So here, experientially, we are exploring that old phrase "to really understand someone's position, we must walk a mile in their shoes". So by this we mean true empathy - really seeing the situation that may be causing another person suffering. Not from our perspective, with our assumptions and conclusions but from theirs. Again, this is another difficult area to examine and it takes time to appreciate the quality fully. We must recognise the different perspectives of the other person in a given situation, without critique. After all, we cannot argue with what the other person is feeling. Misplaced they may be, but the feelings are definitely there and simply telling the person that their feelings are misplaced generally does not remove the feeling. Usually all that does is wind the other person up! So, we have to approach with gentle open-mindedness. After all, if they are suffering, then the one thing you do both agree on is that neither of you want to suffer!

We all have the power of empathy, often what stops us feeling it is fear. Are we brave enough to walk that mile in the other person's shoes? This is why it is called compassion. Because to really enter in, we have to feel their passion! And when we have "enough challenges of our own, why would we want to do that?"

The Magic of Noticing – Andy Spragg

Well, this is what Buddhist practice asks of us. Compassion is an extremely generous act. We are truly walking alongside someone. The Buddha taught us that to be generous is a key to our own spiritual progress. Now, there is something that feels a little odd in the western mind. We know and understand that when we are generous, we do it without expectation of a return. But when we practise generosity from a Buddhist perspective, there IS a return and we are encouraged to enjoy it and appreciate it. If you are truly mindful and fully paying attention in the moment where you perform that generous act. Right in the moment, pay attention. Pay attention to the act of the generosity and pay attention to how you feel. Not afterwards but right in the moment, you will feel a great warming in your heart. This warming is Metta and it is a massive tonic. As Buddhists, we practise generosity and we are encouraged to pay attention to the effect deep within us. So, there is no material pay-back from the other person but there is a massive spiritual payback! And this is so powerful.

I would encourage you, when you are feeling down or depressed or a little disconnected in the world, go out and seek out someone who needs help. And help them. Pay full attention while you do this and see how it makes you feel. Really see their situation, respect their response to it and help them in any way you can.

6.3.4   Sympathetic joy

The third element of Metta. Put simply it is the practice of rejoicing in others' happiness. Mostly we are able to connect with this. Particularly when we consider our families. Of course, we can rejoice when our relatives are happy. A short while ago, my brother and his family were staying with us and his daughter found out that she had achieved her grades in her A-Levels. A gorgeous moment and it is very easy to experience sympathetic joy at times like this. But this area presents us with a much tougher challenge. Picture yourself at work. You work hard all day and you have a colleague at the same level. Then, one day, your colleague is called in to the boss's office and given a promotion. You graciously shake your friend's hand and offer out to them how happy you are for them. But, how do you really feel? What's going on inside. Sympathetic Joy requires great honesty with yourself.

Usually when we consider the word "sympathy" we consider feeling and sharing someone else's pain. Sometimes this is actually easier to do than honestly sharing someone else's happiness and being truly sympathetic of it. Here, we are turning the understanding of sympathy on its head. We are being sympathetic to someone's good fortune. We get faced with the challenge to this element of metta all the time. I think particularly this is more challenging in the west because we are taught to be so competitive here. To constantly strive to be better than our workmates. Our organisations reward us when we go above and beyond what's required of us and we stand out. This is an understandable practice, but it has an unfortunate side effect. It can turn people away and against each other.

It is almost as if the concept of sharing and taking a view of rejoicing for someone else's successes and happiness goes against the grain.

This word joy is also a very interesting word. Sometimes it gets associated with pleasure but the two are very different. Essentially pleasure is driven by the way we react to things external to us. We "take pleasure" in things. But joy is driven internally. It arises internally from our own state of mind. So here, with sympathetic joy, the feeling arises internally. It is true love arising in relation to our response to another person. It is genuine. Not some artificial response prompted by how we "think" we should behave in a given circumstance. It is real and genuine joy.

6.3.5 Equanimity

The fourth element of metta. This is even trickier. Here we are challenged with developing an equal and open heartfelt compassion to all that we come in to contact with. This cuts back into the root of one of the Buddha's first sermons where he talked about suffering, or Dukkha, as he called it in the Pali language. The essence of the sermon was that suffering is not experienced as a result of whatever is happening to us. Suffering is caused by our response to whatever is happening to us. If we can learn to develop an approach of acceptance to life as it transpires, we can let go of the suffering. If we look at the implications of this, we see that many things in our own personal lives cause us suffering.

Metta, compassion and equanimity ask us to develop a level of acceptance towards these things that we perceive as leading to suffering.

Equanimity therefore asks us to see both sides of our challenges, appreciating that they are part of our love and even having a sense of compassion for them when they challenge us. With the things that cause us suffering, we are tasked with appreciating that they are as much a part of our rich life experience as the things which give us pleasure. If we can get to this place, then we stop grasping and desiring those things that we think cause us pleasure and stop pushing away the things that we perceive as causing us suffering. This way we reach a place of contentment and from this, true joy emerges.

So, all this sounds like a massive task. We approach it little by little, day by day. The Buddhist practice for this is called the Metta Bhavana (See 5.6). Here, bhavana translates as "the cultivation of". So, the cultivation of Metta or loving kindness. It is a formal sitting meditation, but it does engage the more creative side of the mind. It takes many weeks to work through, but it is an exceptionally rewarding meditation as it starts to make a change to you and the way you see the world. It truly alters your perceptions of the world around you.

6.4   Entering into suffering

Consider a diamond. Perhaps an odd question when we are talking about suffering. What words come to mind when we think of a diamond? Expensive, hard, sparkling, engagement, cutting, beauty etc. Some of the words are related to how the diamond appears but many of them are associated with what we infer and associate with the diamond. So, this is showing how our mind embellishes what we initially see. What we actually see is something sparkly, transparent, colours refracted, tiny reflections etc. So, there is nothing visibly to do with value or the ceremony of engagement. This is all inferred. We can't even "see" hardness. That is only revealed if we touch the diamond. But when we see the diamond, we envisage the hardness because of the embellishment from our minds. It is this process that we need to go into with mindfulness. We can understand this on an academic level, but we must actually feel the process going on. We need to separate out the perception and then feel the mind embellishing the object.

If we look purely at the visual, then a dew drop has very similar characteristics to the diamond. It is just as pretty and has similar light refracting and reflecting properties. If the diamond was fashioned into a bead, the two would be identical. But if we understood and labelled the dew drop as a diamond, the mind's embellishment would attach value and the nature of hardness to it. With this practice it helps us to see how we mentally react and embellish in all aspects of our life, including the areas that cause us suffering. Our suffering is not as a result of the things that happen to us, it is the result of our reaction to the things that happen to us. It is embellishment from the mind that is causing this.

So, consider the simplicity of a diamond and all the embellishment we wrap around it. Then move on to a rather more complex object - a person. Just think of all of the embellishment we wrap around a person. Even when we meet someone for the first time, our minds start to categorise and make assumptions about that person based on people we have seen before. We start to decide if they are professional, trustworthy, lazy or hardworking, conceited etc and they have not even told us their name yet. Of course, they are doing the same in their attitude to us. When people reveal their prejudices about us, to us, we feel anger. But we do just the same to everyone we meet!

The Magic of Noticing – Andy Spragg

So, the practice of mindfulness here is exceptionally important. Otherwise, we never allow ourselves to meet the true person.

The mind's behaviour is often described as a mirror. It shows us what the mind's idea of the world is, not the actual world. Which is tricky, because the only reason we can perceive the world is because of Mind!

But why DOES this cause us suffering? The suffering we are talking about here is Dukkha. Unfortunately, some people do have to cope with chronic pain in their lives. But this is not what we are talking about here. Dukkha is roughly translated as the general unsatisfactory-ness of everyday life. So, the suffering caused by sitting in traffic when we are heading home from a busy day. The worry caused by a comment made by a friend or acquaintance when we do not know the context or reason. The anxiety caused by the lack of Wi-Fi in our hotel (ridiculous I know, but for some people this is a very serious issue). The process sitting behind all of this is the exact same process as the diamond: the mind's interpretation and embellishment.

So, by practising mindfulness we start to feel this process happening in our minds. We can then bring to bear all of our meditation practice. We spot the embellishment and we spot the emotions that arise as a result. We spot the resultant tension and holding behaviour in our bellies as that emotion manifests. We then work on all this to bring an attitude of softening and compassion to our bodies. More importantly we start to catch our minds as they start to embellish and literally stop the process happening in its tracks. So, we see what is presented to us, rather than our own mirror.

The Magic of Noticing – Andy Spragg

Of course, our meditation is the practice of developing this mental habit of mind-watching so that we do actually do the mindfulness!

In meditation we can use the mindfulness of breathing (see 5.4) to mind watch and notice our reactions to meditation. We are cutting down a lot of our sensory input in meditation, so we are very much simplifying the situation. It is therefore much easier to stay mindful and watch our mental reactions during the meditation. To see how we push things away during the meditation and how this causes us to feel frustrations. To ask ourselves why we cannot make progress. Slowly, through practice we lessen our reactions and when we achieve that we discover the deep bliss of insight and understanding.

6.5   Wholesome, skilful or good vs unwholesome, unskilful or evil

Many religions have a concept of good or evil in them. There's some sort of implication of divine retribution if we don't follow the rules. No doubt the rules are based on compassion. The majority of religions are compassion based. But the Buddha set out an approach to us that shows a way for us to grow spiritually without reliance on a third party. Although, as Buddhists, we don't deny the existence of these supernatural entities, Gods, demons etc. we don't see ourselves relying on them to take us forward or hold us back. So, if we don't have these entities casting judgement does good and evil not exist for us? Well, yes and no. We tend to use different words. Words which are somehow gentler. The original Pali word is – kusala – which translates as skilful or wholesome. The opposite of this is akusala. In the Pali language to generate the opposite of a given word or phrase, we simply say 'a' in front of it.

Buddhism challenges us to approach ourselves in a way which is firm but at the same time gentle.

If we look at this term wholesome from the perspective of the Oxford English Dictionary - **good for you, and likely to improve your life either physically, morally, or emotionally.**

People new to Buddhism often think that to be Buddhist we have to somehow selfless, never thinking of ourselves. But here we have advice, buried in the Buddhist texts, seeming to tell us to concentrate on things that are wholesome for us?

The truth is that it works both ways. When we offer energy out to others in some way shape or form, which is wholesome for them, it is also wholesome for ourselves.

Let's dive in and take a look at an example: the act of generosity. Giving something to help someone else. This is an excellent example to really understand how this works. In Buddhist practice we are encouraged to be generous, either with energy, with our time or even with material wealth if we are able. We are encouraged, in the moment of the generous act, to pay attention. To listen with mindfulness to really understand the full picture, and to see the result of our generosity in the other person and in ourselves.

We do, however, need to take care with the nature of the response here. Because, of course, sometimes conceit and pride arise. We might be thinking to ourselves "look at me, look at what a good person I am."

The challenge that Buddhism presents to us is the challenge of total self-honesty. So, if this type if thinking does arise, we then go into the emotions surrounding these thoughts and ask ourselves "is this wholesome?" This is not easy but if we are going to make progress here this is what we have to do - apply total self-honesty.

Anytime we are looking at these emotional responses and asking ourselves "is this wholesome?" we have to try to feel the answer rather than answering it on some intellectual level. At an intellectual level, we may conclude that conceit is in some way bad or wrong. Then we start to judge ourselves for being conceited. So, we must listen to the dialogue in our heads and stop this kind of chatter before we disappear down the rabbit hole of self-judgement. That will not help us to make progress. Instead, we examine what happens inside of us when conceit arises. Go into the feeling in the heart and the gut and we will feel a sense of remoteness from the person we are trying to be generous towards. We will feel disconnected and perhaps superior. Feel that and notice it. Try to let go of the dialogue that is driving that emotional response and instead focus on other aspects of your response to generosity. Feel the joy in the moment. See the recipient's appreciation and feel your own natural joy. Notice then the wholesome nature of this response. Instead of feeling distant you will feel very connected. Celebrating shared joy between the two of you. This is wholesome.

We can do this with any thought or emotion that goes through us, asking ourselves, "is this wholesome?".

The Magic of Noticing – Andy Spragg

We know in our hearts whether something is wholesome or not, skilful or not. We don't need to be told. Personally, I believe we have an inmate knowledge of what is skilful and unskilful.

In Buddhism we have a guide to help us: The Five Precepts. They should not be seen as a rule book or something to be compared to or judged by. But they do helps to steer ourselves towards a wholesome life. They are -

- Refrain from causing harm or taking life
- Refrain from taking what isn't given
- Refrain from uttering falsehoods
- Refrain from sexual misconduct
- Refrain from intoxicants

All of these can be wrapped up in complex legal structures and lengthy debate held about what is allowable and what isn't. But actually, in our hearts, we know. We need to look at these and what we know of them in our hearts, spin them on their heads and think about the positive side. Think about the wholesome behaviour that sits on the other side.

Many people who encounter Buddhism are in very stressful jobs. They may be very successful, but the job is taking its toll. This is one of those very tough positions to be in, but we must ask ourselves. Is this wholesome? Is it wholesome for me, for my family situation etc. Part of the Eight-Fold Path, the Buddhist structure for spiritual practice, has the step "right livelihood". This way of thinking is key to that step. Is this position or job wholesome for me? Is it taking me forward on my spiritual journey or is it holding me back? Your livelihood does not have to be some high-minded spiritual pursuit. You could be working in an office in an admin support role. Nothing at all wrong with that. But if the working environment is intimidating or confrontational and it is causing you to step off your personal spiritual path, then it is not wholesome for you and you need to look at it.

Meditation practice must be wholesome too. Everything from the nature of your mind during meditation to the physical posture you are sitting in, needs to be wholesome. People often ask me; can I lie down during meditation? I would suggest not. I would suggest finding a comfortable seated position with the spine as upright as possible. It must be comfortable, but your posture should carry a sense of alertness about it. If you finding you are tired, and meditation sends you to sleep then you probably need to take a look at getting more sleep. Otherwise the meditation itself will not be delivering the goods. It is just giving you a nice nap!

One meditation subject that we know is wholesome, is the metta bhavana (See 5.6). This is the practice I would recommend here. As you go through the practice, examine what is going on inside yourself and consider the wholesomeness of your experience. Feel the joy that comes from the generous act of offering your love to someone else, even someone who has wronged you. Often the toughest part of this meditation is step one, offering yourself love. So, feel that sense of compassion in your heart as you offer yourself love and notice how the body responds. Tension eases out of the face, the heart feels as though it is opening. These are all definitely wholesome responses.

The Magic of Noticing – Andy Spragg

6.6   Spirituality and the mind

Sometimes, before we settle down to meditate it is good to just get a view of our state of mind, to know what we are starting with.

Mostly, meditation will consist of lots of sessions where we feel mildly better afterwards but nothing particularly dramatic happens. That doesn't matter. It builds up. It slowly changes us. It is therefore healthy and encouraging, to keep checking in with ourselves.

How do we actually do this checking in? We can look at many aspects of this. One way to help us is to work with what we call the spiritual faculties. There are five of them. They are firstly arranged in to two pairs that are opposites to each other's pairing. So, we have what we call Prajna. This translates to Wisdom. In this state of mind, we tend to be sitting in a cerebral place; academic if you like. It is very much a thinking and reasoning state. The opposite of this state is what we call Sraddha. In this state we are swayed towards faith and a feeling of letting go in the world. Now, hearing this, you may think that from what you have learned about Buddhist practice, this may be the way to go. But actually no. In the extreme of this state, you will believe anything you see or read, happy to go along with it all. Your meditation will not be present. It will be lost in a trance like state. I am not seeking to discredit any other system, but this is more akin to Transcendental Meditation (TM) where we are seeking to come out of ourselves and enter this trance like state.

In Buddhist meditation, this is not our aim. So, we have to balance this out with prajna (academic thinking). The mind has to be engaged and present. But, of course, too much prajna and we will be over-thinking our meditation experience. Meditation will be an academic process rather than one of true experience.

The other two opposites that we experience are Virya, which means energy, enthusiasm. This is incredibly important. It battles against sloth and torpor, sleepiness and laziness, gives us strong intent and keeps us going in our practise. Then we have Samadhi. This is the meditative states of concentration and absorption. Note that this is not the same as prajna. The concentration of prajna is applied thought. Samadhi is applied non-thought. It is a deep sense of presence with the meditation subject. Of course, this is a good thing. But if we have too much of this and too little virja we will be stable but be lack-lustre. Our meditation will not be achieving anything. It will be a static thing without life. Meditation is not empty. One of the outcomes of meditation is emptiness. But this is a realisation, not the experience of meditation itself. Meditation has presence. It is alive. It is a very active, engaged state of non-thinking.

But of course, if we have too much virja and not enough samadhi, we will be fidgety and distracted, not able to focus the mind.

The state sitting in the middle of these four opposites is Smrti, mindfulness. Or rather, this is what is required to balance these other states out. Meditation is the practice; mindfulness is the resultant state.

So, all well and good but how does this sit with spirituality. Well, let us do an exercise. Let us say that there are two main types of spirituality. The first is very grounded, in touch with the earth and the body. I do not have much knowledge of the American First Nation or some of the shamanic systems, but they seem to be very grounded in earthly systems and are very connected with the body. Both these systems practice many approaches to medicine using natural herbs and incantations to help the body. Then there are spiritualities which are more heavenly. Looking up outside of ourselves. The universal nature of experience, if you like. Christianity is more akin to this, I would suggest. Most religions or spiritualities seem to be more one than the other. All have elements of both, but both these elements are definitely present.

So, with this in mind, take a moment to check in with yourself. Ask yourself "what is my spirituality? Is it grounded and inward or universal and outward?" There are no wrong answers here. Both are important and necessary. Don't overthink it. In fact, don't think in the traditional sense. Just feel!

The meditation I recommend working with here is the body scan followed by just sitting (See 5.3). What will be important here is what you do with your internal gaze. Even with your eyes shut you can direct your gaze up or down. Our direction of gaze actually triggers different areas of the brain. Looking up engages long term strategic thinking and seems to hook with ideas on universal awareness. Looking down engages with that grounded nature, short term planning and close concentration. Remember. Both are important.

So, during your meditation, if you feel you come from a grounded nature or spirituality, cast your eyes up in meditation. If you tend to be in a universal, external place, look down. Notice how this affects the mind and the meditation.

6.7   People are landscapes

A Raindrop falls

Will it feed a river, flower perhaps or creature perhaps?
A thought trickles through the mind
Will it feed fear, anger or compassion?
Karma is born
We are a landscape"

A few years ago, now, on Holy Isle, a Tibetan Buddhist Island, just off the Isle of Arran, Scotland, I was running a Tai Chi and meditation retreat and taking some time out to rest. There is a lovely hill in the middle of the island and one morning I took a walk up it. The view from the top is gorgeous. I was standing on top and watching the rain sweep across the distant hills on Arran. You can see the highest mountain, Goat Fell from there and it was looking very dark and moody across there that morning, although my hilltop was in sunlight. Watching the rain and the landscape from a distance like this, it made me realise that I was watching dependent arising in action. For the benefit of non-Buddhists reading this, dependent arising, or pratītyasamutpāda, is the understanding that nothing exists in and of its own right. Everything is the result of some cause and effect. If fact, in Buddhism, each and every moment has this in its very nature. Even WE are the result of dependent arising, each and every moment of our lives. There is no single thing called 'me', just a set of interdependent events, actions and thoughts that create the perception of this thing called 'Andy Spragg'.

I realised that studying this landscape in front of me was a little like studying a person. Just as complex, just as intangible.

A single droplet of rain falls from the sky. Who can predict which way it will go? It may land on hard ground, flow into other flows of water and together form a stream, a river and cut down into the landscape in a very obvious but slow manner. The droplet may land on soil or a plant, becoming absorbed as the plant sends its roots down. The plant itself, becoming part of this rich landscape, the roots subtly changing the soil below. Lichen may be nourished by the water and change the colour of the stone it is growing on. An animal may drink from a pond that the droplet has landed in. Who knows the way that animal may contribute to that landscape?

I started to see all these things within the landscape and the view before me was suddenly more complex and beautiful, but also fragile. I suddenly felt the very nature of change in this landscape at a very deep level. It was at this point, while studying this gorgeous vista in front of me that I started to think about people and the similarities with these thoughts.

When a person stands before me, I perceive what I believe is their character from what is displayed by their appearance and by the limited set of actions that I have witnessed since I have known them. Just like with the landscape, I am misled by my perceptions. I don't see the equivalent of the drop of water.

The Buddha gave us this view of our minds, our thoughts, and how they build our character.

The thought manifests as the word;

The Magic of Noticing – Andy Spragg

the word manifests as the deed;

the deed develops into habit;

and habit hardens into character.

So watch the thought and its ways with care;

and let it spring out of love born out of concern for all beings.

As a Buddhist I believe that my body (yes, body!) and my mind at this point in time is literally the composition of all my previous thoughts and actions. There are clearly external influences that happen, and the Buddha describes how these influences affect us too. But here the message is clear. Each single thought we have goes into our very makeup.

This is just like the raindrops in our landscape. Every thought is like a raindrop and we can never really predict what effect it is going to have on our character.

So, when I study a person, I cannot see these previous influences and I certainly am never going to be able to grasp the rich history that has created this person. Of course, the person concerned, being studied by me, believes they understand their own character. They will have a much richer view than I do. They may even have some knowledge of the "droplets of water" that have taken them to where they are now. This, if you meditate on it, on your own "droplets of water", makes you realise how little you know about yourself and about your own landscape. With practice, you start to dissolve. This is key experience if you are making progress with Buddhism, I believe. It may sound a little frightening, but the experience is actually rather liberating. So, just like my perceptions of the landscape, my understanding and knowledge of the person before me is severely limited. How can I truly know and connect with this person when I view them from a distance like this?

To truly connect with a landscape, we have to walk within it. We can choose not to, of course. But if we really want to understand it, to experience it in its fullest extent, we have to choose to step into it. However, when we do this, we do, of course, have to take the experience exactly as it is. When we walk up the steep hill, it makes no sense to shout at the hill and say, "You are too steep for me, you are making me tired". The hill will not change. When our boots get wet from the wet grass, we cannot actually do anything about this if we wish to cross the field. We simply have to accept it. After all, if the hill was not so steep or the grass was not quite so lush and wet, the landscape would not be the same from that distant view. We must accept it as it is and simply view it and experience it.

Also, and most importantly, if we choose not to enter in, to see things from our distant, limited viewpoint, we may well miss the greatest beauty.

There is a gorge in Crete called the Sumaria Gorge. From the top of the gorge is a beautiful view. But the real gem of this gorge can only be seen when you step down into it and "connect" with the landscape. In order to do this, you have to put your boots on and trek along a nine-mile, dusty, rocky path. Crete is a hot place, so this is no easy task. The truly spectacular part of the walk is almost at the end. Here the gorge narrows to just a couple of metres wide and the river squeezes through this narrow place. The sheer

The Magic of Noticing – Andy Spragg

height of the cliffs and the dramatic nature takes your breath away (if you've got any left after the hike!) But, if you had not connected with the landscape and entered in, taking everything as it is, you would never see this stunning scene and truly appreciate the beauty of Sumaria Gorge. You would miss the real beauty.

I believe that connecting with people is a little like this. We must be prepared to connect. But in order to do this we have to take them exactly as they are. There will be hills to climb and hot, dusty pathways. But we must just notice them, see them, every aspect of their character. This way, we find their most beautiful aspects and we will be surprised and delighted by the rich connection we then have with them.

There is no need to understand how each individual raindrop has shaped the landscape. We simply open all our senses and connect. Step in.

These days there seems to be so much analysis done on people. We are categorised and analysed. There are so many therapists out there figuring out why we are the way we are. Why do we need to know this to connect with each other? I don't believe we do for a minute. There is nothing to fear with connecting with people. We should celebrate our complexity and our individual nature.

Simply connect. There is nothing else to be done.

6.8   Guilt vs remorse

We have lots of guilt here in the west. I am unsure where this comes from, but it feels as though there are aspects of our society which increase feelings of guilt. In fact, it has almost become the norm to constantly compare ourselves to others, feeling guilty when we don't come up to par. With a global populate of 7.9 billion people we will highly likely "fail" if we do this. Of course, we tend to compare our lives to the lives of public figures. Film stars, billionaires, global entrepreneurs and seek to live up to our perceptions of their lives. Is that really wholesome?

There are three parts to an emotion. There are the thought processes that contribute to and justify the emotion first. These might be based on all manner of inputs from our mind. They could be triggered by our deeply held beliefs or prejudices. They could be driven by our desires, our aversions or our delusions (our personal view of the way the world is, or the way we believe it should or should not be). This is a complex area and often we cannot unpick everything that goes on in the mind.

Then there is the raw energy of the emotion. This is usually felt in the heart area or the gut, but we can experience it right through the body. How often have you, after a period of extreme stress, felt that every bone in your body ached?

Then there is the third part of emotion which is the triggered action that comes out of it. The way we present our self and the things we say.

Usually, all of this, leads on to further emotion. With guilt, this tends to spiral us down and down into a complete pit of potential despair.

I advise you to get in touch with the energetic side of the emotion, to feel directly and to try not to focus on the thinking. When we focus on the thoughts, this actually feeds the fire of the emotion.

The Magic of Noticing – Andy Spragg

The thoughts that come up will be full of justification for how we are thinking and self-judgement. If the emotion is desire based, when we focus on the thoughts, this can lead to stronger and stronger craving and on into pure lust which takes us over. When the thoughts are aversion based, ill will and hatred comes in. Anger. Delusion is complex and can lead to both of these effects but also anger and fear.

Guilt, of course, arises in us where we perceive that we have done something that is not wholesome in some way for someone or some situation. When we feel this, it is extremely easy to drop in to self judgement. So with mindfulness, the approach here is to notice and let go of judgement. We simply examine what we can do differently. Not in retrospect but in from this point forward. This is of course what we call remorse. In Buddhist thinking, guilt is an unwholesome emotion, but remorse is wholesome. Remorse sees change that we can make to ourselves. Guilt is a wallowing self-pitying emotion which just takes us down. Remorse is a positive, building emotion that takes us up on the spiritual ladder.

6.9   Chaos, the teacher

The natural order of things is chaos. Possibly a controversial statement and we could discuss it at length. But let's take a look at nature in the raw.

The woodland embodies chaos. When you look out on the woodland, the trees have not grown in any ordered way. They are all unique and different in shape and they have grown in a very random fashion. The woodland floor is covered with thickets of brambles and fern, completely impenetrable to walk through. The birds are singing. Their song is a chaotic cacophony. But it is so beautiful for all this chaos! This is the natural world. Chaotic, without order and absolutely stunning.

However, if we tune in, we can also pick out patterns in the birdsong. Similar sounds from the various species come through. The birds and their song have evolved this way so that they are able to identify mates, warn each other of danger and possibly even help to find food that is relevant to their species.

There are tracks through the forest that humans have made. Without these, as I say, the forest would be impenetrable. Chaos is the natural order of things but all the species occupying the woodland, without question, and to some extent, evolve to bring some form of order into their lives. We humans have taken this to the furthest extent. Our ability to plan, design, see risks and bring order from all this chaos is phenomenal.

The real illustration of this is of course found in our cities. The modern human city is a complex set of interoperating processes, functions, rules, roles and incredible electronic and mechanical devices. Our manipulation of energy allows us to drive through the design and build of the city and all these things are intermeshed and co-operating with hugely complex systems of interdependence. All designed and built by humans. Nature invades the city of course. Dust and dirt, soil and creatures of many types creep in but we push them back out. In places within the city we choose to groom nature to our design, to bring order to it and turn it into our parks and gardens. These parks and places are beautiful, but they are manipulated into that state by human-applied energy. Take that energy away and the park will quickly start to revert back to its natural, chaotic, state. Just look at how much energy you have to apply to your garden to keep it looking "nice".

I do not intend to give you the impression that I am criticising these human achievements. There are some who believe that everything man-made is bad. This is not me. I love our cities. My wife and I spent a day in Paris one spring and it was stunning to walk along the banks of the Seine in the sunshine and see the tended fruit trees in full blossom. Our parks are gorgeous and the creativity and design that has gone into them I find wonderful. But chaos is the natural order of things and is with us always.

To change tack a little now, mindfulness practice is a practice! In sitting we learn to open up and see things as they are. Our relationship with chaos and nature is a key aspect of this. Living in a city, looking closely at the world around us, we perceive the chaos. Sitting in meditation, the first place we find chaos is in our own minds! The practice is to just notice this first, to simply perceive the nature of our minds, exactly as they are. In my early experiences of meditation, I was amazed how chaotic my mind was (and actually, still is!). Thoughts, emotions, memories and desires were all jumbled up and tumbling over each other.

When I first came to Buddhism, it frustrated me. These days, that's just the way it is, like the woodland. My mind has not changed; I have just learnt to accept it the way it is.

Then there are people. How unique and different we all are. Such wide-ranging opinions on the same topics. Such different approaches to the same challenges. Step off the busy street, enter

The Magic of Noticing – Andy Spragg

the modern office and observe for a while. Here you can see this chaos in full flow, and of course it is people that make it this way. The energy we apply here to bring order to the chaos is in the way we generate job and role descriptions. Describing the way people should behave in different situations. But we are still, underneath, infinitely complex as human beings and we don't entirely fit into these formal categories. Then these roles and categories have complex jobs to do, all designed to bring order out of the chaos. But the chaos is still there and sometimes the grey areas in these categories and roles cause our complex processes to break. When this happens, the individuals owning the roles involved often get criticised, chastised and even dismissed from their jobs.

But I say again, I am not against all this. These human abilities to plan, categorise and manage leads to amazing things. Our organisations are very necessary. I draw on the modern hospital. Saving lives where the ultimate expression of chaos is threatening to take hold. In a hospital, in order for it to deliver its task, these roles are vital. But when something goes wrong, if we are being mindful, we will understand the influence of chaos here and perhaps be a little more compassionate and gentler in our reactions to our colleagues.

I perceive that it is this chaos and our desire to bring order that sometimes lies at the heart of many of our problems and suffering. The modern world needs order and control. The city requires great energy from us to keep the chaos at bay and maintain order. The place outside of that control and order is a fearful place for many of us. There are many people these days who are thrown into anxiety when their mobile phone goes wrong or the shops are

The Magic of Noticing – Andy Spragg

closed on a bank holiday. In most of us this anxiety may be fleeting and passes quickly but for others it can become a real problem, leading to unskilful behaviour, anger and violence and in some people developing into deep mental health issues. Interestingly there is a great deal of evidence to suggest that the more organised and structured a country becomes the more the general population suffers with mental health issues. The more developed we become and the more we drive to bring order to the chaos, the more we suffer. Very strange and very interesting! We truly are a fascinating species.

I believe that this suffering is primarily from fear and this comes from the fear of disorder and the unknown influence of chaos and the desire to drive order. You can see some real hard evidence of this in our supermarkets. A couple of years ago a fight broke out in our local supermarket just before Christmas Eve. Literally a physical fight. There was only one of the "special" turkeys left and two ladies had planned their whole Christmas meal around having that turkey on the table. Bizarre behaviour from these two well dressed, normally well-mannered people. But it is this kind of extreme behaviour, when the stress of a desire to have planned order in our lives, gets tested by the natural chaos that is always sitting underneath.

The more complex we make our plans, the more the chaos will force its way through, because that is the natural order of things.

With our approach to people the challenges really kick in. Because we are so beautiful and complex, we act in so many ways and respond to this complexity. Clearly our responses cannot be truly predicted, because by its nature, chaos is infinite.

The Magic of Noticing – Andy Spragg

So, of course, to cope with this we do the human thing. We bring in labelling and categorisation. To try to make order out of the infinite nature of humans we give labels. Here's a few – male, female, rich, poor, Buddhist, Christian, Catholic, Protestant, gay, straight, democrat, republican, ugly, thin, fat etc. The number of categories we put people into are huge and of course growing all the time. Some of those listed above are relatively modern. Again, it is this behaviour, this natural human behaviour, that leads to suffering. We form views of how we believe people are and should behave based on the category we have just put them in. When they do not behave in exactly the way we believe they should, for the category we have chosen, we react with confusion, anger, fear and stress.

But still we suffer as we make our human world of process and order more and more complex and chaos bites back even more viciously. What should we do? Simple. Become mindful.

No need to become a Buddhist. That is just another categorisation, after all. But just by being mindful and seeing things as they are, we can become aware of the beauty in the chaos and relax with it. With people, we can see them for who THEY are, not the category we put them in. This way we become more tolerant and respectful of their views and approaches. In our modern world we can appreciate the cleverness of human design but not fear the chaos of nature that is always there.

In this way our meditation truly becomes a practice with chaos as the teacher.

The Magic of Noticing – Andy Spragg

You will find no better teacher of mindfulness than the chaos in your own life. But like any learning, in order to learn from the teacher, you must listen. Here, our listening approach is to meditate and become mindful. Meditation is just another form of Listening. Listening and noticing.

So, the meditation I recommend here is to first notice the influence of chaos in your own mind and develop an attitude of accepting it. Afterall, it is from this chaos that our true nature of creativity and individuality emerge.

Using the meditation – Just Sitting (See 5.5) we can explore the chaotic nature of mind and learn to accept that nature. This is just the way the mind is. We have to soften into the experience and try not to "expect" an ordered calm mind. To make progress with meditation, we have to first accept the nature of mind.

6.10 We are farmers of our own mind-field

I have talked before (See 4.4) about our the mind can be viewed as formed from three main parts. One, the manas, the thinking mind if you like. Two, our store consciousness. Memory, of you like. Three, awareness, the Gardener. The part of the mind that can watch the other two parts at work.

Here, let's take a look at the store consciousness and its nature. We can view it like a field of earth, with seeds resting in it. The seeds are below the earth. We can't see them, but they are there. Our store consciousness has seeds scattered within it and these have been laid down by our lives, ready to be nourished and watered.

The Magic of Noticing – Andy Spragg

These seeds in our store consciousness can be one of three types: wholesome, so they are helpful and supporting to ourselves and the world around us; unwholesome, so they are not helpful; and a third type which we call indeterminate. Depending on a given situation, the indeterminate type could be wholesome or unwholesome. How can this work? Well, let us take a look at a particular seed lying in there and see what happens. It is one many of us have in this day and age - self-critique. Actually, this particular seed can be both good and bad. It is certainly healthy to take a look at ourselves and see how we can better ourselves. But, in many of us, particularly in the west, this goes too far, and we end up in a position of self-loathing. I see this one coming up so often in people these days and it seems to be getting worse.

These seeds have been planted in our store consciousness by our lives. It may be our society that has planted them, our parents, or our life experiences. In the case of self-critique. Certainly, in me, it was planted by my parents, encouraging me to take a look at myself and better myself. But they did this very skilfully, giving me encouragement all the way so I didn't end up in a position of self-loathing. But our society and life seem to push the other way. Images in the media, on TV and in on social media show us what our life "should" be like. This triggers this particular seed in some of us.

So, this depicts how a seed takes form. It manifests in the mind as a mental object when nourished in the right way. Without noticing this going on through mindfulness the seed will become stronger, manifesting ever more powerfully in the mind.

The Magic of Noticing – Andy Spragg

Anger is a good one to examine. It is in all of us and ready to manifest given the right circumstances. When I was a teenager, I was angry a lot of the time. I think the world was not going fast enough for me. I was not sure what I was looking for but whatever it was, it was not happening quick enough. It took a tumour in my hip joint and then the subsequent practices of tai chi and Buddhist meditation to calm me down. The seeds are still there but I notice the potential for the nourishing of them these days, so they don't manifest so often any more.

There are other seeds in our mind that we all have that we can choose to nourish. Compassion, gratitude, forgiveness and joy. When we focus on these in any given situation, we are directing the nourishment away from the unskilful seeds. These seeds are definitely there and always available for cultivation.

There is a therapy which asks the patient to "get in touch" with their anger. To shout and scream and perhaps beat up a pillow. Actually, I don't consider this a very wise therapy. This will nourish the seeds of anger.

I'm not suggesting we suppress our anger and pretend it isn't there. We should understand It. Sit outside of it, noticing when it is being nourished and then apply mindfulness to it. Breathe into it. Let it go. As always, the magic is in the noticing. Doing this is not the same as suppressing the anger. Here we are simply letting go of it.

Let us now connect the dots with Buddhist practice, the heart of the Buddha's message: the four Noble Truths. This essentially spells out that our suffering all comes from our mind. This has

The Magic of Noticing – Andy Spragg

three main drivers; our desires, our aversions and our delusions. Each of these three areas will have very strong seeds in our mind.

I love the analogy of the field. If we water this field in a haphazard manner, then there will be areas of the field where the water will naturally settle and here the weeds will grow. If we really want to nourish individual plants then that is what we must do. We must concentrate on those and let the unskilful weeds wither and die off. It is no surprise that in Buddhist psychology, the guiding light of awareness that sits outside the thinking mind, is often called the gardener.

In section 8.6 we look in detail at a particular area of teaching in Buddhism, the law of conditionality. But I will touch on it here as it is very relevant. The Law of Conditionality says that nothing exists on its own. Everything arises from the conditions that create it. Nowhere more so is this important to understand than in our own minds.

Our mind is our world! Our world is very much the way our mind presents it to us. We can understand this from the simplest level. If we have a negative state of mind, our view of the world will be very negative. We will see risk and suffering, sadness and pain everywhere. We will draw into ourselves to try to protect ourselves from that world. However, if we have a positive state of mind, we will see joy, rich compassion, life and we will connect with it.

So, our state of mind has been delivered and built slowly. Those seeds planted in our store consciousness are dictating our state of mind and therefore revealing to us our world. If we wish to change this, it is not going to happen overnight. The field that we have to nourish and weed is large, having been laid down over many years. So, we had better get to work, with mindfulness. Purely through the power of the mind's gentle awareness we can start to notice how those seeds are being nourished. It will be hard work.

To begin to understand the interplay between our store consciousness and our life, we can use meditation to develop a habit of mind watching. The more we practice drawing back from our thoughts and seeing them as just another experience flowing through the mind, the more this approach will kick in during our daily lives, and we will be able to see our wholesome and unwholesome thoughts and how those may lead to action. So, the mindfulness of breathing is a very powerful meditation for this (See 5.4). However, we can also deliberately plant some positive seeds in meditation with the practice of compassion – Metta Bhavana (See 5.6).

6.11 Delusion, superstition and reality

One of the roots of suffering, the Buddha taught us, is delusion. To understand delusion, it is worth taking a look at these three words – delusion, superstition and reality.

In Buddhist practice they are seen as being related to each other but in conflict and they can occur at a macro or a micro level. From the most trivial of influences in our day to day thinking to very major contributors to our sense of self. As we delve into this area you may see that these are influencing us constantly, every minute of the day.

The Magic of Noticing – Andy Spragg

Delusion and superstition can be seen as connected. Essentially synonymous with each other as they arise because of the same factors. But in practising with these three words, I find that reality cannot exist in the same moment as these two. Or rather, we cannot experience reality at the same time as we experience delusion and superstition. The two appear to be mutually exclusive of each other.

Delusion is a very broad term. The definition, according to the Oxford English Dictionary - a firm and fixed belief based on inadequate grounds, not amenable to rational argument or evidence to the contrary, not following regional, cultural or educational background.

But this does not quite cut it from a Buddhist perspective. It is a little too closed and aggressive. Let me try to put it across from another perspective, from Buddhist Psychology.

Mind (not brain, to be clear) can have many mental states. The Abhiddhama, an ancient Buddhist text, written in the 3rd Century BC, lists 52 of them with a whole bunch of sub-states.

Knowing all those states really doesn't help this discussion much! But it does broadly categorise two main states that the mind can be in, that of perceiving and that of creating. At any given moment, it can be in one of these states. Either perceiving or creating.

When the mind is perceiving, it is taking in information through the five senses, through what we call the sense doors in the mind.

When it is creating, this is an internal process, generating new mental sensations. We have to remember here that the mind is the sixth sense in Buddhist thinking. It has this ability to generate internal mental objects which are the sensations for the mind as the sense organ. This generation process may or may not be based on or related to what is being perceived from the external facing five senses. It will be constructed from objects found in what we call the store conscious.

The store conscious can be seen as a store of everything that has gone before. So, it is a great deal more than memory. We have in here, our things which we are consciously aware of and some that we are normally not. We have faiths, beliefs, mental habit, phobias, fears, indoctrinated thinking etc. Some of it we will have developed and laid down directly ourselves; some may be inherited from others.

You can view the body and mind as not separate so the body is also part of the store conscious and contributes to the whole process. The age of the body, previous injuries, energy levels all contribute.

For example, when I am sitting on my sofa and considering what I will do on Saturday morning, if I am old and tired, the thought of playing football will probably not arise! My creative process will probably take me somewhere else.

This sets out the view of the mind from a perspective of Buddhist psychology. It is not neuroscience. It is a model of mind which seems to work for us, to help us practise mindfulness and meditation.

So, coming back to our three words, delusion, superstition and reality. Delusion and superstition arise because of the creating side of the mind. To all intents and purposes the mental objects they create, don't really exist. They are the products of the creating state. They feel very real as they bubble up in the sense organ of the mind, fed by our store consciousness.

So, investigating this requires a great deal of self-honesty and diligence. If, for example, the mind is creating a mental object because of a deeply held belief in the store consciousness, this is going to be a very difficult area for us to work with. But if we can work with it, we can ease suffering. Trauma, for example, lodges deeply in our store consciousness. The mind, when it experiences sense objects which connect up with the experience of the trauma, will be delivering up graphic mental objects relating to the trauma. (See 6.2) Trauma will not be easy to work with and at times, professional psychotherapy will be needed. It's important to understand that mindfulness and meditation are not psychotherapy. They are a tool for all of us to work on mindfulness and meditation. If a person has long term deep mental challenges, professional help should be sought. Mindfulness and meditation are for all of us.

There is a big implication here. Should we be letting go of our beliefs? If they potentially cause delusion should we find a way to dispel them from our minds? Of course not. That is not the purpose of this exercise. The practice is to just see the influence of these things on our everyday perception of the world. As always, the magic is in the noticing. We are using this particular aspect of mind to develop mindfulness and meditation. To remove a veil from our view, to draw it back so that we can view the world, we

The Magic of Noticing – Andy Spragg

first have to see the veil. This is the practice - of seeing and noticing through meditation and mindfulness.

But at the same time, as we practise, we have to approach it with an attitude of open, seeking, interested Mind. Not a mind that is dismissing things deliberately because they "may" be delusions. Instead, we approach them in a positive light. What can I find, what can I feel, what can I perceive? And at the same time, we pay attention to our mind state. Is it just perceiving or is it creating?

This practice is far from easy. Because the mind is a sixth sense organ, even the thoughts themselves are sense experiences which can be perceived. Because it is the mind, it feeds these perceptions back into the whole process. A recursive process if you like. Activating more mental habits, drawing from the store consciousness and creating still further! It is this cycle we are seeking to step in to with our practice. By simply noticing, through mindfulness, we do exactly this. But we do it with a sense of compassion, gentleness, interest, enquiry and fascination for our mind.

For meditation, we can use the body scan to understand how the mind introduces expectation into the feelings we experience. Are we really feeling those sensations in the body or is the mind introducing expectation and visualisation? Then we can move to the breath and notice perhaps how the mind interferes. Thinking it should deepen the breath deliberately. (See 5.3 & 5.4)

6.12 Where is my mind, what is my mind?

How do we go about exploring the mind? We perceive the mind, with the mind.

This might sound like we are going to disappear down a rabbit whole of recursive confusion. However, using meditation, this is perfectly possible to do.

Here we are going to explore the nature of mind. What the objects floating through it are like and what IT is like in its own right. It is important to note that when we talk about mind here, we aren't talking about brain. The brain is a physical organ. Mind is our experience of, well, something. Maybe consciousness, maybe awareness. Often, we fall into a trap of trying to understand the science behind how something works. So, we get drawn into the neuroscience behind the mind. Yes, that is extremely interesting, but it does not do anything to help us develop our awareness of Mind. In fact, it can result in quite the reverse. Because of our mind's ability to interpret and create, when we hear the science, there is a strong possibility that this results in expectations in the mind and we go looking for and even imagining these expectations. That is not what we are doing here. We are looking for pure awareness. What is our experience of mind?

When approaching this, we start with the body. Why? Well, when we go into experience of Mind, we find that that Mind is not just in the head. You can take your awareness, hence your mind, down into your body. Feel the tingling in your toes. So, the first step is to study how to do this. To search through the body with pure awareness. This has an immediate benefit. It brings us fully and completely in the moment. When we focus on sensory experience, the mind cannot be elsewhere. It is not day dreaming, worrying or planning. You are forcing it to concentrate on one thing alone, slowly training the mind to stay in the mind. You will find the mind wanders. But every time you notice this behaviour you are actually making progress, building a little bit of mental habit. This builds up over time and you will find you can keep the mind concentrated for longer.

But it is so important to approach this with a sense of gentleness and friendship towards yourself. If frustration or disappointment come up because your mind is wandering, then you need to soften into those feelings and bring that sense of gentle friendliness to bear. Noticing the frustration, ask where it materialises as a physical feeling in the body. In other words, making even your frustration a part of your meditation subject!

The body is the first field of mindfulness and we discover that the mind exists right through the body not just in the head.

Then once we are grounded, centred and sitting in the present moment, we adjust our focus to the mind itself.

With practice, using meditation, we can slowly train ourselves to become mindful of the stream of consciousness. Picking up the nature of mental objects as they manifest in the mind, sooner and sooner. Noticing how we initially react to the sensory experience of a mental object and noticing how the mind starts to embellish the experience.

Left to its own devices, the mind will entirely start to feed itself with mental objects. Habit kicks in and encourages the creating abilities of the mind taking us deep into delusion.

Before very long we have totally lost touch with the outside world and mind is going crazily recursive and generating mental object on top of mental object. It sounds crazy but this is our usual experience! Wrapped up in our thoughts, we do not notice the world.

Through meditation practice we can develop a habit of noticing this process going on and draw back from it. Breaking the cycle of this experience we start to become aware of the experience itself. Work with the "just sitting" meditation and experience thoughts as they manifest in the mind. Think of them as containers of stories. Thoughts exist in the real world as they are mental objects in the mind. But the stories they contain do not necessarily exist. They could be created by the mind and are entirely false. This is a little like movies. Movies exist in the real world. We can go to a cinema to see a movie. But the stories within the movies are entirely fictitious. When we are sat in the cinema watch this movie which certainly exists on the screen in front of us. We get drawn into the story and become part of it (if it is any good!) Thoughts are like this. Practice "just sitting" (Section 5.5).

6.13 Bias

Although not strictly coming from Buddhist practice, I'd like to take a look at a couple of biases we humans have and how our meditation can help us to see these influencing our lives and start to balance them out.

These biases are often talked about with mindfulness meditation because it is mindfulness that allows us to see them occurring.

We all have biases in our lives, even our choice of clothes or car or, in fact, any time we have choices to make. If we step outside of the direct process and take a look what's going on, we will

The Magic of Noticing – Andy Spragg

inevitably discover a level of personal bias. And that is just fine. Of course we have bias. In meditation, we can work to see if there is any basic bias there that is coming up.

But I think it is healthy, every now and then, to work against a bias. To actually see what happens. To experience tension arising as a result.

When we have a bias, it is like a comfort habit. When I come home, I like to kick my shoes off, maybe pour a glass of wine and relax with a good book. A bias feels a little like this. It is a comfortable space. A couple of years ago, my wife and I decided to run 100 miles in a month. It was October. Rainy, dark evenings and we would get home and have to run four or five miles. Way outside of our comfort zones!

Working against our bias feels a little like this. We should not be deliberately uncomfortable when we practise our meditation, but we should apply a little effort and sometimes step outside of our comfort zone. The cushion is a safe place to do this. It is very unlikely that we will get cold and wet while meditating, but we can put our minds into similar situations that take us outside of our comfort zones.

It is healthy for us to work in this way as working with bias is very similar to working with craving and desire. We have to notice first and then consider how we pull ourselves back from the bias, using our meditation subject to not allow ourselves to be drawn in.

We can look at two main biases that we all have and that influence our lives.

The Magic of Noticing – Andy Spragg

6.13.1 Negativity bias

As humans, we tend to:

- Remember traumatic experiences better than positive ones
- Recall insults better than praise
- React more strongly to negative stimuli
- Think about negative things more frequently than positive ones
- Respond more strongly to negative events than to equally positive ones

Why do we have it? Where has it come from? Well, the fact is we have evolved this way and during our evolution, it was a very useful trait. As humans, specifically Homo Sapiens, we spent almost 200,000 years as hunter gatherers, a staggering amount of time. Our modern civilization is only a couple of thousand years old and this technological, modern age only about 100 years!

During our time as hunter gatherers we faced many dangers. So, this bias is probably best illustrated. Imagine a hunter out on the plain. He approaches a bush, and there are ripe juicy berries on it. He needs those berries as they are a rich source of natural sugar. So, he approaches. The bush shakes. That is all it does. At this point, this hunter gatherer turns and runs. It might just be a stray breeze causing the bush to shake but he sprints away leaving the berries. Why? Well, there may be a tiger in the bush. Better to escape the tiger and live another day. With this kind of unconscious, instinctive, biased behaviour his ancestors have survived to procreate. Those that didn't flee will have sometimes had berries, but they may also have been eaten by a real tiger! Missing a meal is hardly likely to kill a human, but a tiger certainly

The Magic of Noticing – Andy Spragg

will. So, the bias has evolved through evolution because it has naturally led to those humans with that bias to pass on their genes. Those without the bias may well have got lucky but, statistically, those with the bias will have been more successful at surviving. As a hunter gatherer, there are many dangers, and a healthy dose of negativity bias will take those genes forward.

Roll the clock forward 190,000 years to hear in our modern day. We live in a very safe world. Not many tigers. Here in green Somerset, I'm more likely to encounter a cow! But it will take many more thousands of generations to undo that negativity bias in me. It is there to stay for a good while.

We all experience this bias every day of our lives. A colleague makes a comment in the office which is innocuous and means nothing. But we read the negativity into it and drop down into suspicion, which produces inappropriate emotion and then we act it out.

The negativity bias can have a profound effect on your relationships. The bias might lead people to expect the worst in others, particularly in close relationships where people have known each other for a long time.

For example, you might negatively anticipate how your partner will react to something and go into the interaction with your defences already on high alert. Arguments and resentment are often the results.

When it comes to relationships, it is valuable to remember that negative comments usually carry much more weight than positive ones. Being aware of our own tendency to fixate on the negative is

The Magic of Noticing – Andy Spragg

important. By understanding this natural human tendency, we can focus on finding ways to cut other people a break and to stop expecting the worst.

In meditation this bias also arises. We can find ourselves being critical about our own lack of attention. Not noticing how long we've been present. Just noticing how the mind has wondered.

Focus on what is going well in your meditation. Feelings of contentment that arise perhaps. The reason meditation helps to combat negativity bias is because of its focus on what is actually happening rather than what the mind thinks is happening, or what the mind is imagining might happen.

The negativity bias is very powerful in us, but once you start working with it, it is also rather obvious. Use the mindfulness of breathing (See 5.4)

6.13.2 Confirmation bias

There is another bias that hides itself away. Much more subtle, it sits in the background influencing us. Its success at this is due to the fact that it doesn't necessarily make us feel bad or cause us to suffer in an obvious way. This is the confirmation bias.

Where do your beliefs and opinions come from? If you are like most people, you honestly believe that your convictions are rational, logical, and impartial, based on the result of years of experience and objective analysis of the information you have available. In reality, all of us are susceptible to a tricky problem known as a confirmation bias. Our beliefs are often based on paying attention to the information that upholds them while at the same time tending to ignore the information that challenges them.

The Magic of Noticing – Andy Spragg

A confirmation bias is a type of cognitive bias that involves favouring information that confirms your previously existing beliefs or maybe other biases.

For example, imagine that a person holds a belief that left-handed people are more creative than right-handed people. Whenever this person encounters a person that is both left-handed and creative, they place greater importance on this "evidence" that supports what they already believe. The person feels comfortable with what they are witnessing because of the bias. This individual might even seek "proof" that further backs up this belief while discounting examples that do not support the idea. Perhaps thinking that a right-handed, creative individual is perhaps a bit of a rare anomaly. Maybe even they don't see in their world, creative right-handed people!

Confirmation biases impact how we gather information, but they also influence how we interpret and recall information. For example, people who support or oppose a particular issue will not only seek information to support it, they will also interpret news stories in a way that upholds their existing ideas. They will also remember details in a way that reinforces these attitudes.

Unfortunately, we all have confirmation bias. Even if you believe you are very open-minded and only observe the facts before coming to conclusions, it is very likely that some bias will shape your opinion in the end. It's very difficult to combat this natural tendency.

That said, if we know about confirmation bias and accept the fact that it does exist, we can make an effort to recognize it by working

The Magic of Noticing – Andy Spragg

to be curious about opposing views and really listening to what others have to say and why. This can help us better see issues and beliefs from another perspective, though we still need to be very conscious of our confirmation bias influencing our view.

It is imperative that we get to grips with this. My personal view comes from the heart of Buddhist practice, and the focus on the alleviation of suffering. The three main components of suffering are craving/desire, aversion and delusion. Confirmation bias sits right at the heart of delusion. Essentially, the mind is not seeing the way the world is. It is altering the view to suit its own bias.

So where do we go with meditation? Well, bias also arises in meditation, but in a different sense as sloth and torpor. Our mind actually veers towards things that confirm our bias. In meditation we are essentially taking all sensory input out of the picture, so our mind starts reaching out for things that sit within our bias. A lack of focus on the meditation subject emerges and we have to redouble our efforts. Working on the hindrance of sloth and torpor will help us to ignore the pull of our bias and stay focussed on the meditation subject.

Little by little we soften the hindrance of sloth and torpor, enjoying the interest in the meditation subject in its own right. Not needing anything else. A contentment to sit with the breath, exactly as it is. (See 5.4)

6.14 Human being not human doing

This is a well-known saying, but what does it mean? How do we come at this? If the years of the COVID-19 pandemic, 2020 and 2021, have taught us one thing it is that we have to work to survive sometimes. Those who were in work had to work harder than ever and those who were not had to work hard to find their next job. Not many of us were able sit back and relax.

We also have duties and responsibilities to our families. This puts additional pressure on us because we love them and want to care for them.

So, what do we actually mean by this phrase? Human being not human doing? It clearly does not mean just letting go of our responsibilities. If we are going to live in the modern world, we have to find another way. I will, obviously, come at this from a Buddhist perspective, which means - Mind.

Let us talk first about human doing, which is actually our usual state of play. In Buddhist terms, this means mind active and engaged in thinking. We think about many things and, of course, we have to think. We have to plan; we have to get creative and we have to remember. All functions of our incredible mind. But we do not have to do this all of the time!

Before we discover this wonderfully transformative activity of meditation and mindfulness, we think that we are our thoughts. We think that they help us out of difficulty, make us money, bring us love. It is only when we start to meditate, we come out of this fog and start to realise how much of our life just happens. We fight against so many things when we do not need to. This fighting causes us stress and anxiety because of our desire to control our lives. Take a look at the previous section 6.9 – Chaos the Teacher to get an insight into where the suffering may come from.

If we can just let go of this desire to fight and control, we can relax into, essentially, what is. Of course, that desire to fight and control comes from our minds. Some years ago, a Japanese soldier was found deep in a forest in Japan. He thought the war was still happening about 40 years after it had ended! He hadn't noticed that everything had calmed down!

This is what human "being" rather than human "doing" is about. But we cannot just do this at an academic level. We have to find a way to be vigilant to the mind; to see when it drops into the trap of "doing when there is no need. It is no good expecting that we can just experience this peace when we are sitting in meditation.

Meditation is where we do the graft of developing new mental habit. It is hard work and like any worthwhile practice we will have good days and bad, frustrations and joy. It is in our daily lives where we need to find peace no matter what is going on in our daily lives. Meditation develops mind habit which then comes through in our daily life.

A common trap that people fall into is believing that meditation is some form of spa exercise. Something we do once in a while, legs crossed, fingertips touching, to relax. Perhaps after yoga or some other form of exercise. In my experience all this brings is brief respite. As soon as you exit the sports hall or spa and go back to life, you start "doing" again.

Now, studying meditation will not stop you from having a career. It will not stop you earning a good salary. But it will make you realise that you do not need to be "doing" so much to achieve the same. You can stress out about the next promotion and try to influence or control it. Or you can just relax. Let it come. Work hard and diligently, yes, but while you are doing that "be" rather than "do". If you work in this way, you may also get a better perspective and a realisation that the promotion is not right for you.

It was my meditation practice that brought me to the realisation some ago that the career I had been blindly following just was not for me. I am a great deal happier now even though I am working harder than ever and earn far less money. I have enough. And I am being, not doing.

So, how do we develop this habit? Simply by learning to mind watch. On the cushion we learn to let go of thoughts. To not follow them. They will undoubtedly come so we notice them. It is through the noticing that we are able to let them go.

We use awareness of mind to keep a sense of vigilance. The just sitting practice. (See 5.5)

6.15 Ritual

The well-known Zen Buddhist phrase "the finger pointing at the moon" refers to the means and the end, and the possibility of mistaking one for the other. Our practice in Buddhism has many forms and methods and they are very important as pointing fingers, but if we forget what they are for and they become, so to speak, the goal in their own right, then our progress is liable to stop. And if it stops, it regresses. On the other hand, there are those who say with considerable pride, "I don't want fingers or methods. I want to see the moon directly, directly . . . to see the moon directly . . . no methods or pointing". But in fact, they won't see it! It is easy to fall into the trap of believing we can reach some enlightened state by letting go of all, but I have found in my practice that some level of structure is needed here, some kind of guidance to follow; signposts along the way and indications of what might be incorrect paths.

So as always, that lovely simple piece of advice that the Buddha gave is even applicable here. Take the middle way. In order to do that, we need to be mindful even of our reactions in this area.

Ritual appears in so many aspects of our lives and we can use this as an opportunity to practise our response to it. For example. We can see ritual in our everyday conversation. Someone gives us something. We say, "thank you". Now, I'm not suggesting that we start being impolite. Rituals have emerged over many generations, and they are as embedded as our evolved physical characteristics. But, as always in all of Buddhist practice, the magic is in the noticing. Here we are taking our mindfulness down to another level. We are watching our personal interactions with people and with the world around us. Just spend a day noticing ritual in your own life. It could be simple things. When my wife and relax and sit on the sofa in the evening, I always sit to her left, in "my space" on the settee. That is ritual. So, my advice is have some fun. Spend a day studying your own ritual in your life. It teaches you a great deal about yourself. Look at speech patterns, the way you respond to similar questions. Look at physical ritual. The way you brush your teeth perhaps. Play around with it. Mix it up. See how it feels when you go against some of the ritual. Perhaps do that on the second day after watching it on the first.

The Magic of Noticing – Andy Spragg

Ritual makes us feel comfortable. It is like an old friend that we always fall back on. There is lots of embedded habit.

Why practise in this way? As an example, we can examine fear. Much fear arises from a fear of the unknown or the fear of the chaos (see 6.9) in our lives. But there could be part of it caused by the challenge to the personal ritual of our lives.

So, we can start to practise with this to learn how to relax into the situation. As always, we come back to the Buddha's simple message. We don't suffer because of the things that happen to us; we suffer because of our reaction to the things that happen to us. Examining our own personal ritual and experimenting with gently changing it in safe ways, shows us how we can relax into these changes and discover that our life does not fall apart when we do experience pressure on our personal ritual. It just changes our lives a little. We will feel tension, we will feel resistance. We study that feeling, notice it in the body and the mind, and practise physically and mentally relaxing into it. We can then start to widen out and work on some of the bigger change that is going on in our lives.

Of course, we can do this in meditation. Meditation practice over the centuries since the Buddha's death have, in some areas, become very ritualised. Whole books these days are now published which set out specific paths for meditation. The Satipathana Sutra, the writing that sets out the Buddha's primary advice on mindfulness, covers the main areas for practice, but it does not set out a strict approach. If anything, it is very open in its nature.

When I lead meditation, I tend to set out an idea of a path. I tend to start with the body scan. Then I typically suggest a word to accompany the breath to help develop soft concentration. Then I may suggest dropping the word and drawing attention to a spot in the body where the breath can be deeply experienced. This has been my practise for many years because it works for me. You must find your own practice. Your own ritual. The only "advice" I would give is to keep in mind the aspects of mind that typically pull us away - desire, aversion and delusion. Keep your concentration centred on experience and avoid the influence of delusion when the mind overlays the experience with potential falsehood. Because that overlaying may, itself, be the influence of your own ritual.

You may well ask, why change the way I meditate? You might perhaps prefer using some involved visualisation to helps to relax you, de-stress you and take you away from your current problems. Before I became a Buddhist, I was taught a lovely meditation. It had me visualising lifting up, flying out the roof of my house and drift over my local town like a bird. It gave me a great feeling of openness and release. Ok, nice. But actually, it was only after practising Buddhist meditation for some time, that I began to realise that meditation doesn't always have to be "easy" and "nice". We physically exercise to better our bodies. It may be easier to sit on our sofa with crisps and our favourite drink, but we know that exercise is what our body needs. Yes, sometimes we must rest, but if our habitual practice is resting on our sofa all the time, we are going to become weak and Ill. The same goes for our mind!

The Magic of Noticing – Andy Spragg

Unfortunately, I believe that many religions have allowed delusion to creep in, becoming ritual, and this ritual has replaced the original message of the religion. Many years ago, I went to church with my parents. The men were coming in and taking off their hats as a mark of respect and this had become a ritual that people were following. The scowl one woman gave her own husband because he forgot to take off his hat was awful. She looked at him with such scorn. I knew that man. He was not a bad man; he had just forgotten to take off his hat! He was a regular attendee at church and a believer in God, but he forgot to take off his hat and got treated like a devil!

A process of enquiry and investigation is so important here. Be creative about how you approach the task.

We go through the fields of mindfulness, but I want you to investigate it in your own, unique way.

1. The body.
2. The breath
3. Feelings and emotions
4. Mind and mind objects.

Remember though, the only thing I recommend is to keep in mind the roots of distraction and ultimately suffering; desire, aversion and delusion. Notice when the seeds of these areas come up. See when they start to appear, let them go and re-focus.

The ONLY ritual I advise is regular practice.

6.16 Love, joy and peace

These sit beyond emotion. Emotions emerge from our dualistic view of the world. The dualistic view leads us to the place where we need external things to ensure our happiness. We push away external things that cause us to fear. Emotions like fear and happiness emerge because of the roots of suffering - desire, aversion, delusion. However, love, joy and peace emerge from inside us. They come up out of a calm mind.

Peace and tranquillity have been felt by all of us. When we sit on a quiet beach and listen to the waves lapping and smell the air, we feel it. The problem is we then associate the feeling with the experience of being by the sea. The idea of being by the sea then becomes a desire. We "want" it and believe that the only way we will discover that tranquillity is to be by that seaside again.

Actually, in doing this, we have just recreated that duality. The tranquillity is not dependent on us being by the sea. It is by creating that calm peaceful place in our minds. We can do that without the seaside.

When we lose that duality, we are completely in the moment, connected to ourselves and connected to all around us.

Contributing to all this is our mind tone. Our mind's tone essentially defines the way our world is. If I have a mind tone which is jumbled, troubled, scattered and perhaps angry, this will be the world I occupy. I can try to blame how I feel on external things, but it will not do me any good. I will be fooling myself. Using meditation changes this mind tone. If my mind tone is open, receptive, gentle and compassionate, this will be the world I occupy.

This duality is where our suffering comes from. This dualistic view of the world leads us to look for external things for our happiness. We cannot find it because that is an artificial view for how happiness works. Happiness bubbles up from inside, when we have peace and tranquillity inside of us.

This is why we meditate. We are learning how to change our mind tone; how to develop that feeling of peace and tranquillity from inside ourselves.

There are many people that go on yoga or meditation retreats time and again and believe that the only time they can find peace is on retreat. Again, this is just another version of duality, relying on something else to give us our peace. Now, I am not suggesting we do not go on retreat. Retreat gives us a good opportunity for practice in a quiet environment. But we must understand that we need to be watchful that the retreat experience in and of itself, does not become a new source of addiction and therefore suffering. Are we depending on a retreat to find peace? If we are, there is a problem. Because to find peace, we do not need to go on retreat. We can discover this peace in the comfort of our own home, sitting in meditation.

One of the most common questions I hear is "can anyone recommend a good meditation app for my phone, as I can't seem to settle down to meditate". Again, this is bringing duality into the picture; an assumption that an app is going to give us the peace we are searching for. Apps, just like retreats, are good starting points. They kick off our practice. But, at some point, we must free ourselves from them and learn to meditate by ourselves to find how to generate that feeling of inner peace and tranquillity by our own practice.

But how do we do it? How do lose that duality? Well, we need to develop a habit of noticing when it is occurring. When we are producing feelings of separation. Noticing our craving behaviours, we can ask ourselves what it is actually that we are craving. Noticing when we are blaming external things for our suffering. Examining our reaction to the things and using meditation and mindfulness to change that reaction. We slowly learn to capture these mind objects as early as possible, when they are just seeds of thoughts in the mind.

We must practice, because we are not going to learn how to achieve a change in mind tone by accident or by relying on external things.

Change your mind tone with the Metta Bhavana (See 5.6)

6.17 Reaching our highest human potential

Buddhism is an interesting spirituality in that it does not look for any form of external agent, a God, if you like, to make progress. The belief is that we can make spiritual progress entirely through our own efforts. It doesn't deny the existence of God or gods, but it also does not rely on them.

It is very practical in its approach. It understands that there is birth, there is life and there is death and that none of us can escape this. So, in our exploration of the spiritual, we seek to go beyond this, beyond the suffering in our lives.

But interestingly, it is the very nature of our lives that gives us the vehicle for our transformation. It is in the midst of our struggle that we make progress.

I do not believe that Buddhism is the only route to achieving highest human potential. All the main religions have the same goal. Strip away politics, radicalism, competitive human spirit and all the other complexities that us humans bring to the party and you are left with the same thinking. But I think the key difference is that Buddhism acknowledges that very human nature, embraces it, uses it, to make progress. It is our very human-ness that actually allows us to make progress.

What is it we are trying to achieve? What is "the highest human potential"? It is certainly beyond the mere physical, although there is no doubt that physical feats are impressive. Our athletes accomplish amazing things. When we talk with those athletes, they often express that through their training, they achieve higher mental states. It is their ability to concentrate and overcome the pain associated with their training that allows them to achieve their physical goals. So physical pursuits, we can see, are another way to develop ourselves towards.... something? We do know, however, that no matter how hard we train our bodies will become old and eventually we pass on. No amount of physical training will avoid this. So, my view, is that our practice, in terms of spirituality, does go beyond this. As an aside, it is definitely a good idea to look after our bodies and do some physical exercise. Any pursuit will be stronger if we have a healthy body!

The Magic of Noticing – Andy Spragg

So, we do of course move on to our minds. This is why I have such an interest in meditation. Essentially, in meditation we are becoming familiar with the workings of our own mind. It is going to be a lifetime's work and it will require a great deal of personal effort. But little by little we transform ourselves. Normally, when we think of working with the mind, we think of it in some academic sense. Improving our knowledge, making our concentration stronger, making our memory/work better etc. This all may well be side effects of meditation, but that is exactly what they all are, side effects. Because that still doesn't feel like achieving a highest human potential. Buddhism goes beyond this. Tasking us to let go of the ultimate piece of grasping nature. The desire to hold on to self. When we truly do that, we let go of that ultimate need. To protect our ego. Our conscious core. The ego, because of its nature is always reaching out for things that will nourish it and pushing away the things it believes will damage it. But, because of the nature of mind, it often gets these views wrong and it causes suffering to itself and to other minds.

By meditating, we become very aware of the nature of mind. What it does, how it behaves. Essentially, we develop a habit and ability to step back from our mind and its stories and see it at work.

6.17.1 Developing a concentrated mind to carry us through

When carrying a hot cup of tea through a crowded room, you need focussed attention on the cup but still be very aware of the goings-on around you, stepping gently, with care, so as to not spill the tea. It is more important to reach the destination with all the tea still in the cup than to arrive quickly.

The Magic of Noticing – Andy Spragg

This is exactly the type of concentration we have in meditation. It is relaxed, unhurried. Our focus on the meditation subject but still with awareness of our surroundings, our body, our thoughts. We experience it all, but our focus is still on the subject.

When we do this, we gradually develop an ability to relax into the task. Yes, there are distractions. But those distractions are all the result of mind. Think about it. You are sitting meditating on the cushion; it is late in the afternoon and a smell of baking comes into the room. Your mouth starts to water, and you notice the hunger in your belly. You think you can force the hunger to go away or stop your mouth watering. Of course not. But you can stop the next thing - the mind cutting in, thinking about what it is smelling, embellishing the experience. Instead, firstly, relax into the experience. Focus on the smell. See if you can identify any undertones, any constituent parts. Go into the smell! Make the smell part of your meditation. Make it a friend of your meditation. Take a look at the hungry belly. Is it really that hungry? Are you about to starve to death? Of course not. Go into the hunger. Where is it? What is it? Is it pain? Or is there a pleasure to that experience? Most importantly relax into all of this.

Slowly, working in this way, we start to carry this type of practice into our daily life. We soften into the hardships. When we do this, we also notice more clearly the support that those around us, give us and also their hardships and their needs. Bingo, we have just taken a step towards a higher human potential.

6.17.2 How do we handle distractions?

Here, I am talking about external distractions. We view things happening outside as the cause of our distraction. We see or hear them first, that is extrospective awareness, then we perhaps bring an element of focus to them, that is extrospective attention. As we continue to work, we begin to really see that the things that happen are not what distracts us, it is the mind's reaction to them that causes the distraction. So then, our understanding becomes introspective. We will naturally start to see what the mind is doing. We need to learn to use this in meditation. With our focus on the breath, we have introspective awareness which is continuous. Then we have introspective attention which is momentary. We look at the mind's reaction to an external stimulus before we come back to the breath. Little by little, even this behaviour fades and we are able to sit with our focus on the breath and outer introspective awareness "policing" our mind to notice those early seeds of distraction.

Slowly, little by little, mind loses its power over us. Its ability to distract us becomes diluted and this is where we truly start to let go of the notion of self, because we start to see and understand that that notion of self was just the mind's behaviour to distract. The mind focuses on the things it believes nourishes it and push away those that it believes take away its power.

Read any of the great texts from the religions of the world and you will see the same, only "Mind" is given a different name. Demon, devil, evil spirit etc. Here, I do not practise with the view that the things that distract me are evil, not even wrong, just human. Not necessarily wholesome though, and sometimes unskilful. So, we practise on the cushion and gently develop our habit of mind watching, to let go of this dualistic aspect of mind. Then the shackles come off.

The Magic of Noticing – Andy Spragg

6.18 Renunciation - acceptance and letting go

Often, when people encounter Buddhism, they see those aspects that seem rather austere. They will hear that the practice is all about understanding suffering. That we have got to perhaps eat just one meal a day, let go of our belongings, give up worldly things.

These are misunderstandings. The practice is not about this. A key part of the practice is renunciation. We understand this to mean refraining from, holding back from, giving up something altogether. Of course, to do this, we would have to mentally make the choice to do this. Again, like all of Buddhist practice, the practice starts and ends with Mind.

Remember, Buddha said that we can be a prince in a castle but still achieve enlightenment if we understand the suffering that comes from grasping and desire. But even if we are a monk, residing in a monastery, if we do not understand that suffering and we crave and grasp, we will not make progress. So, it is not the action of renunciation itself; it is the mental intent that matters. How do we practise this? Two words are key here. Acceptance and letting go. They are two sides of the same coin.

Working in meditation, I have heard many people talk about acceptance and letting go but I am not sure they know what they really mean.

What are we letting go? Well from a practical and probably fairly superficial level, this could relate to material possessions. Many of us have more than we actually need in this day and age and recognise that we need to declutter.

The zen master Shunryu Suzuki Roshi said renunciation is not giving up the things of the world, but accepting that they go away.

But I would like to take this a little deeper and move into the mental side of this discussion. The opposite of letting is holding on, grasping or indeed craving. Grasping is when we have something, and we do not want to let go of it. Craving is wanting more. It is this mental behaviour that causes a great deal of our suffering. Much of our suffering comes back to this and much of our unskilful behaviour is born out of it. This behaviour also hides itself well and can become ingrained habit, even grasping or holding on to negative mental states. I have known people who have been depressed but have displayed a definite grasping nature to their depression, not wanting to let it go.

I am sure we have all known people who have been generally angry. Often these people will actually fear letting go of their anger in case it somehow diminishes them.

Even spirituality can produce grasping and craving behaviours. There are plenty of examples in history where a religious leader imposes stringent rules on their followers to feed an ego, keeping the flock in check and aggressive behaviours are displayed when members of the spiritual community decide to leave. What was love, suddenly becomes anger and the person is potentially shunned.

What matters, as always, is our mental response to our surroundings. Having said that, it is definitely simpler to practise with less of the clutter around us.

The Magic of Noticing – Andy Spragg

But we can take this a little deeper still. Many of us unfortunately suffer with physical illness. We are all getting older. Even those born yesterday have already started to age! Our physical being is another area that we have a tendency to grasp on to. We face anxiety and even depression when our physical being is facing a long-term problem. Some of us even worry over our physical bodies when they are in fine health. Michael Jackson's mental health problems seemed to have been born out of a desire to live forever. So, we also need to practise with this and explore our relationship with our bodies, to see where craving and grasping are creeping in. We see plenty of craving behaviours in the world. The whole of the cosmetic surgery industry has been established around this. It is clearly good to maintain a healthy body in order to achieve our fullest potential (spiritual or otherwise) in life. But, we will all age and we will all die so we do have to come to terms with this otherwise we will become mentally or physically ill as a result of the grasping and craving at some point.

Some of Buddhist practice sounds incredibly pessimistic and difficult but in fact it is immensely practical. After all, we know that not one person in the entire history of mankind has avoided death. (Although of course the Christians amongst us may debate this) Then there are our relationships with people. Here we are looking at the affect that the other person has on our life and the effect we have on theirs. Love is when you are thinking … "how can I make you happy?" Attachment is when you are thinking … "why aren't you making me happy?" Whether we are talking about close partners, family or even friends, this still applies.

The Magic of Noticing – Andy Spragg

Grasping and craving start at the superficial and run deep. Their opposites are accepting and letting go. By accepting, we acknowledge that nothing lasts for ever and everything changes. Nothing is static so we have to accept that we cannot keep it and we must let it go.

So, the final area to investigate here is the letting go of self. This is the most challenging area in Buddhist practice. We attach to the image of self, hard and fast. Buddhist practice, particularly the six-element practice (see 8.5) reveals to us directly the lack of a permanent self. The strongest element is the conscious mind. But when we directly investigate the nature of the conscious mind we do not find self there. And we slowly discover how to let go.

Our approach to studying this starts with meditation. I will say again, we practise on the cushion, and we make progress when we get out into the world.

The practice of renunciation, whether we are on the cushion or not, is to actually take notice of our mental response to things and noticing when grasping and craving are creeping in. Then to look at how we offset that nature with acceptance and letting go. Every minute of every day we will get an opportunity to practise this so we will not be short of practice time!

We can explore our grasping and craving with our meditation. Noticing our desire for the noises from outside to go away as it may make us more concentrated, how we wish we could sit in perfect full lotus like the Tibetan masters we have seen on TV. Noticing our desires to keep our concentration focussed in a zen

The Magic of Noticing – Andy Spragg

like state and never wavering. The magic is all in the noticing. Use the mindfulness of breathing (See 5.4)

The Magic of Noticing – Andy Spragg

Chapter 7. Meditation contemplations

In the previous chapter I explored some specific Buddhist psychology; a way of thinking which is perhaps different to our usual mode. In this section we start to look into what happens as a result of meditation. This is commonly known as insight. Essentially, we start to notice things about the world, about us and about our relationship with the world and other people, that we had not noticed before. We are starting to notice, actually, the way the world is. This discovery is also known as "wisdom". Buddhist wisdom is not an academic thing - it has to be experienced. We cannot think our way through to insight. It is discovered. I sometimes think it feels a little like looking at those magic eye pictures that were popular a decade ago. A random set of coloured dots on the page. You would stare at them and suddenly a three-dimensional picture would leap out of the page. Sometimes it would take a while and it was almost as if, when you relaxed your eyes, the miracle happened! Insight/Wisdom is just like this. It hits you with its obvious nature and leaves you asking, "why didn't I see that?"

So, this chapter may help you to start to experience some of this in your own meditation. You can introduce these sections as contemplations before or after your own meditation.

7.1   Calming turbulent waters

We will always have turbulent waters in our lives. Sometimes they may be choppier than other times, but they will always be there.

In Buddhist practice we learn that we can't push these challenges away. We cannot structure our lives so they do not occur, no matter how hard we try. Yes, it is prudent to work towards ways to lessen the impact of difficulty. We have a compassionate duty to others and to ourselves for this, but we cannot take these turbulent waters entirely out of our lives.

Buddhism in this respect is annoyingly down to earth. It is not going to take our problems away. In many ways it simply changes our perception of "the thing".

So here, in working with this aspect of life, we go right back to basics with meditation, to see how we cope with these areas of life that challenge us; not only cope but also open our arms to all aspects of life. In Buddhist practice we call this equanimity - the ability to appreciate all sides of life. Equanimity is a key goal in our practice. But you do not have to become a Buddhist to appreciate its benefits. Often, we allow things to affect us, to get under our skin and push our buttons. Someone says something that we rightly or wrongly interpret as an insult. A business deal does not quite work out. These types of things can end up colouring our whole day. Even when we have nice things planned, sitting in the back of our mind is the incident. At two o'clock in the morning, we wake up thinking about the situation and cannot get back to sleep.

The practice of equanimity helps us to stop pushing these aspects of our life away. They happen and they either do or do not affect us. We actually have a choice whether we allow them to affect us. But it is hard work and takes practice.

A large part of this is about the ego. The ego is a part of us which demands attention. It demands feeding with things that it thinks will nourish it and it demands to be kept free of things it thinks will weaken it in some way. However, it is quite often wrong! Often it finds ways to justify the things it is desiring but these often will not actually be wholesome for us.

That word "wholesome" (See 6.5) is a key word in our practice. We can ask of any situation, is this wholesome, for ourselves and for the people around us?

These things that challenge us WILL continue to happen to us. So, the guidance that Buddhism offers here is not about finding ways to avoid these challenges all the time. It is about learning a gentler approach, for ourselves. A way to calm those turbulent waters caused by the challenge in our lives. A way to change our reaction. In the case of social media, yes, we could unlike our friends or even come clean off it. But that would be a shame on both counts. Social media is a great way to keep in touch with friends and family. So, to come off it because of one comment is a shame. (Of course, if you are regularly getting these kinds of responses to your posts it may be worth having a think about what you are posting!)

In exploring this area we are essentially learning stillness. Using meditation to calm the emotional turmoil that comes up in this type of circumstances. Setting aside what has happened, we look at the result. Not the result as in the story, but the result in our own bodies. What is going on? Emotions have a physical response in the body. Adrenaline, blood pressure, heart rate, breathing all go up and those waters get pretty choppy. I do not think anyone would think that this is a nice place to be. We do not want to feel

The Magic of Noticing – Andy Spragg

like this. We want to feel calm, relaxed, rational, open minded, peaceful. So, this is what we work on directly with meditation.

It is difficult, because our default reaction is to try to rationalise the situation and when we do this the mind supplies us with the justification for how we are feeling. All this does is ramp up the emotional response because our ego says "Yes, I'm right to feel like this!"

We work on building a habit of mind and body watching. It is very much about habit. When we are getting hit by the challenge in our daily life, unless it is habitual, we will forget to tune in and notice our emotional responses and our thoughts that trigger and get triggered by these responses. If we have habit, we tune in to the sensation in our bodies that is caused by emotional response and we learn to settle it.

Meditation on the breath. Settle. (See 5.4)

7.2   Developing the enquiring mind

One of the challenges many people find when they come to meditation is keeping a sustained practice going. Initially, many find a sense of real excitement with meditation. They are starting something new and they have strong emotionally engagement.

But then this feeling wanes. It all gets rather boring!

It is certainly one of the key hindrances that the Buddha taught - sloth and torpor. The meditation lacks energy. It is sleepy and uninteresting.

So, what do we do about this? After all, it is just the breath! We breathe around 30,000 times each day. So, we are already pretty familiar with the breath.

We need to cultivate a deep interest in our meditation subject. When we are interested in something, we become engaged in it, even absorbed in it. But again, how do we become interested in something that is so familiar and mundane? In truth, the breath is far from mundane. We just need to go into the detail of it.

A key consideration here is that with Buddhist meditation, we are talking about direct experiences through our senses (where the mind is also a sense organ). So, we are looking at the meditation subject through the five senses and then seeing how the mind itself reacts. Stepping back from thought, it is by seeing how the mind is reacting and responding to the meditation subject that we start to lift the lid on some of the mind's inbuilt mental habit. It is this process that gently produces transformation for us, taking us forward with our spiritual practice. We start to see that the thoughts and mental processes do not have such power over us. They do not run our lives and they do not necessarily tell us the truth about the world.

So, the enquiring mind is not the thinking mind. This is absolutely key. When we turn our minds to thinking, the thoughts themselves take us away from the meditation subject. We are thinking instead of seeing. Instead of experiencing the breath, how it is and feeling how this affects our mind, we will be thinking about it.

The Magic of Noticing – Andy Spragg

So, we are going to look at two analogies which help us to get a feel for the nature of the enquiring mind.

First, the river. Not a young river but an ancient river as it flows down a valley. Just picture that for a moment. Picture its slow gentle laziness. Imagine for a second, if that river had an emotional temperament, what would it be like? Try to feel that a little. As that river flows, it explores all the gaps it finds. It goes in to all the tiny nooks and crannies, even between the grains of sand. It leaves nothing unexplored that it encounters. It makes no specific choices. It does not decide that a particular channel is a bit boring and not bother with it. It just explores. It does not judge that things are not worthy of its attention. It explores. After all, it never knows what it might find. It does not have a motivation to do this. There is no desire to glean knowledge or achieve anything. It just does it.

It is important to think about the aged river, not the young river. The young river is noisy, crashing down the course and disturbing things. We need a slow, wise river which sees the nature of what it is flowing through rather than the silt it is generating. Initially, in our practice, we may well see silt. The thoughts that come up. But as our practice matures, we will become settled and see clearly through to the river bottom.

There is something about the strength of this way of thinking too. A river has such great strength, but it achieves its task, if you like, in a very easy way. When objects get in the way, it doesn't get angry or frustrated. It does not try to bash them out of the way; it lazily moves around the object. Over many years, yes, it may wear its way through things, but it does this with huge patience and perhaps of course, if it had a mind, it would find out even more about the riverbed or the objects within it. It is drawn by gravity and it is happy to follow it.

We can think of our meditation in a similar way. With the strength and direction given to our meditation by an enquiring mind we can steadily head towards our right view.

The second analogy I would like to give you is the very young child. What is the nature of the mind of that small child? The adult's approach to enquiry is to think about the object, asking questions about it, making conclusions and learning. There is nothing wrong with this process by the way. We need to understand our world from an academic level. But that is not meditation, mindfulness or connection. The child's experience is very different. A very young child does not even know about learning. The child is open eyed and open minded. They are naturally enquiring. They want to know EVERYTHING, but they are not worried about why. Therefore, they do not make assumptions or overlay with belief. They just experience.

This is the mind we are looking for. As we grow, we lose this natural enquiring mind. Our thoughts and our ego start to take over. We see others and we have the desire to compete, to conform. We see sensual objects that please us and we want them! We form plans for how to get them. In this way we start to close ourselves off and separate from the world. The river is an inherent part of its landscape. We have a tendency to separate ourselves from our landscape, to see ourselves as separate.

The Magic of Noticing – Andy Spragg

So how do we get back there? How do we reconnect with the mind of the small child? We start simple. We use the breath as our meditation subject, and we remain vigilant to our mind and its tendency to barge in and take over! We mind watch.

Let me give you an example. Let us imagine we are seated in meditation, feeling nice and relaxed and we are watching the breath. We suddenly notice that our breath has become very deep and slow and we wonder if perhaps by slowing the breath a little more we can go in deeper. There it is! The mind has interfered. That is the thought that has come in, that we need to catch, notice with interest and let go. We can even use our enquiring mind to take an interest in the mind itself. "Oh, look at that, how my mind is trying to direct me to slow my breath." Trying to interfere. We are interested and amused by its behaviour and we let it go. We do not want to dam our river or change its course. We want it to just explore.

So, we use the body scan and the mindfulness of breathing. (See 5.4)

7.3   The mind, the mirror

As we deepen our practice, we start to notice the way Mind influences our view of the world. We start to see that we do not actually "see" the world with our eyes. Our eyes are just a ball of jelly with some rather clever lenses in front. Without Mind, they do nothing. The magic happens when the eyes send the signals they have received through to Mind. Here, perception happens.

Of course, this then leads to the potential for embellishment. Because this is what the mind does. This embellishment happens almost instantaneously and is driven by the full weight of our Karma. What do we mean by this? In Buddhism, karma means action. Karma vipaka is the result of our action. This manifests in the world we come into contact with plus our own minds. Essentially, every time we do anything, we are forming mental habit to a large or small extent. When these actions, under similar circumstances, are repeated, we deepen the habit, so that, like ruts in the road, we drop into the same thought processes and therefore follow on to repeating actions.

So that sets the scene. The world we encounter through our five senses and the mind then embellishes this, based on our karma - all our personal history, to put it another way. This results in us essentially forming expectations for how we believe the world should act around us. When it does not follow these arbitrary "rules" we have established, we react with fear, frustration, or anger. If things do not go exactly as we had planned, we resist. We see this most clearly in our interactions with other humans. We expect people to act in a way which we have set in our minds. When they do not, it comes as a surprise, and we react with emotion. In our work, we create role descriptions to try to push people into these boxes of expectation.

There is no bad thing about this. We have to do this in order for our organisations to function. We need a level of expectation, of course. I am not saying there is anything wrong with our desire for order. But I am saying that this is where much of our suffering comes from. Essentially our mind delivers up for us a mirror reflecting our desires, aversions and delusions. Even the most grounded of us get frustrated if we cannot make that purchase that we want, do not understand the behaviour of the person in front of us or feel fear when our job is not going the way we think it should. So, the mind presents itself. We do not see the world; we see the mind's view of what it thinks the world should look like.

Gradually, because in meditation we turn our attention in on mind itself, with mindfulness, we can study the nature of our own mind and see it displaying this mirroring behaviour, dishing up a view of the world. We see it even displayed in the mind! So, our mind forms a view of what mind should be like, then we discover that it is not like that and the realisation dawns.

What do we find? Rather than finding a nice, ordered structure to our mind, that is perhaps our expectation, thoughts jumble over each other. They seem to fire off in a random fashion and come up from nowhere. Often people coming new to meditation are worried that they can't "shut the thoughts up". We have to learn that to let ourselves truly go into meditation, we have to accept the mind exactly as it is and just let it play. After all, it is this chaotic nature of mind that makes it such a wonderfully creative thing. We would not want to stop that. We just have to accept it and let it play, while we quietly concentrate on the meditation subject. If we resist the nature of mind, we will not be able to find peace in our meditation. When we accept the nature of mind, we also start to learn to accept the nature of life and the challenges it presents to us.

7.4   Am I present now; was I present a moment ago?

Even though my tradition isn't Zen, I do draw a great deal of interest and inspiration form the practice of the Koan. The koan is an unanswerable question and there are many examples. Here is a well-known one – What was my face like before my parents were born? It makes you think.

The koan is a contemplative practice alongside of our meditation and in my practice, I have found it very useful to explore some of the aspects of meditation. So here, we can take a look at this simple koan, "Am I present now, was I present a moment ago?"

This simple koan is a great deal bigger than we, at first glance, realise. The first thing that the koan introduces us to is this idea of an "I". So even before we've started exploring the meaning behind the koan, we can start with this. Remember that Buddhist practice is all about seeing things absolutely as they are, with total honesty about the experience. So, when we ask this simple-looking question, we have to look deeply into our experience. Even the experience of I, when we consider it, starts to become complicated. What we have to do here is not fall back on any formal teachings, any doctrine, any expectations of any sort actually. Buddhism and meditation are not about following things with blind faith. They are about our honest personal experience. So, when working with this koan, we start with nothing. Literally no-thing! As we meditate, we look into the experience of self. The body scan is a very good place to start and we look at our physical being. As we move through the body it is our awareness that is perceiving the body. So straight away this gives us an honest challenge. We are perceiving the body, feeling the sensation and aware of the subtle energies flowing through the body. But the body is the perceived. It is the focus of our awareness and attention. Who or what is doing the perceiving? Go into that. That is where your contemplation should sit when you consider this koan and start to look into the subject of I.

The koan then goes deeper. It starts to introduce the time element into the experience. Firstly, the subject of a now. How long is a now? The implication is that it is the immediate now. So, in your contemplation, try to get into that space - the smallest period of time. After all, even your perception of something a quarter of a second ago, is in the perceived past. It is not now. The koan asks, am I present now? But every time we try to look into our experience, we find that we are looking at the immediate past. We are not looking at now. So, we are therefore exploring the second half of the question, was I present a moment ago. We are not actually looking at now. Travel further into this because it really is a fascinating area to experience in your meditation. Look at the now and see what you can find. Remember, do not travel into it with any science, doctrine, belief system or learnt mental behaviour. Just go in entirely from the perspective of experience. What does your honest, bare awareness tell you about your experience of now?

The world starts to melt away when we do this. In my practice I find it deeply restful. When we ask a question of ourselves, there is a brief moment when the mind decides on its direction and the way to tackle the question, where there is a space. The question has been asked but nothing has arisen yet. Go into that space and look at your experience there. Ask the question of yourself, in your mind and then take a look at your experience immediately afterwards. What is your awareness seeing?

The Magic of Noticing – Andy Spragg

All of this can bring up emotions. Have the courage to be fully present, to truly let go of the future or the past. We hang on to thinking about the future and the past because perhaps we think that if we do not plan and prepare for the future or we do not learn from the mistakes of the past, then the wheels will really come off and life will not go well for us. But actually, if you look honestly at the experience of now, you will see and understand that the only reason things go wrong is because of delivered thought. Out of thoughts arise words and out of words arise actions. It is our thoughts and actions that take us off the rails. So, actually, the safest place we can possibly be is resting here on this cushion, being fully in the moment and just experiencing. Meditation is an exceptionally safe place, so we can therefore let go with confidence.

The practice of the Japanese Zen koan has a great deal in common with another great practise from the Buddhist tradition, the Mahamudra. Mainly a Tibetan Buddhist practice, it grew out of traditional Indian Buddhism and is described in the Pali Canon. It means "the great seal" which can in turn be translated as the "great truth". Actually, that is a very grand term, but the truth of the matter is that we can experience its teachings today by just sitting on our cushions and being fully in the moment. So, the practice is just that: letting go of every piece of mental obstruction such as beliefs, doctrines and expectations and just sitting fully in the moment.

I suggest you start with the body scan (see 5.3). Work through the body and experience the sensations but also, as you travel through, just be aware of awareness itself. See the watcher who is experiencing the sensations and study your experience of that.

Then move into a period of just sitting. Am I present now; was present a moment ago?

7.5   What can I find behind my mind?

Another Zen koan for you. I love Zen koans.

Questions are a really powerful way to kick off investigation and enquiry. Koans are deliberately unanswerable. They create "feelings" for answers rather than a specific response.

One evening, my wife and I were watching a documentary by Brian Cox, The Universe. Brian was strolling along the beach and posed the observation that there could be more stars in our galaxy than grains of sand on that beach. Straight away it gives you a feeling of immense scale. You do not even try to figure out how many grains of sand we are talking about here. You just feel the scale.

Another koan that we can work with in a similar way and the one that I often come back to is "What is it like behind my mind?"

It captures the essence of part of a meditation practice. It has all the hallmarks of enquiry about it, but it isn't asking for an academic answer. When we use this koan, we simply experience.

So, when we talk about mind here, we are not visualising something. We are talking about what we can directly experience. Of course, what we can experience are the mental objects as they arise. We can look at these as they arise, see what they are, let them go and experience what is behind them. This is what the koan is

The Magic of Noticing – Andy Spragg

asking us. Sometimes, it is much easier to go searching for something in order to let it go. In order to let go of something, perhaps we have to grab it first. With the mind, when we deliberately go in to strive to empty it, it fills with thoughts! Instead, in meditation we deliberately examine the nature of those thoughts. Not the stories they carry but the experience of the thoughts themselves. When we do this, they seem to evaporate.

I am no neuroscientist, so I do not actually "know" how thoughts work. But I'm pretty sure if I read up on it, I would discover that they are essentially electrical impulses flowing across synapses, activating neurons. But, instead of reading and listening to these words, I simply experience. When I do this, it certainly does not feel like the scenario I have just described. It could not be further from that. So, knowing what is physically happening, does not really help me with answering the experience I'm looking for in the koan. When we go into a koan, we are not doing science. We are doing meditation. Just work with your experience. There are no wrong answers. It is, after all, your personal experience (but watch out for delusion, the mind's tendency to create something). So, go into the experience of a thought. What is a thought like? What does it feel like? Find a thought. See if you can stop it in the mind. See if it has a front or a back. In this way, you may discover, as I have, the lack of power they have over us.

In our mind, we have a particular type of mental object that is often arising - desiring, reaching, grasping or wanting. These are described by the Buddha as one of the roots of suffering. These roots we shouldn't envisage as bad, or evil. Wanting, desiring or grasping are necessary traits if a species is going to survive on earth! But it arises in situations where it is necessary. Evolution is a greedy master, constantly seeking to push an organism to the top of the tree. However, we as humans can now choose to be more mindful about what we do. To notice where these deeply embedded evolutionary traits are not wholesome for us or for the world around.

Our ego drives this. By ego, I do not mean some pompous thing, simply the sense of self. At some level, the ego believes that it will be nourished in some way by the thing it craves.

Exactly the same as a thought, a desire or a craving is a mental object and it can be investigated in the same was. We can experience it arising in the mind. Buddhists practise renunciation, not because we believe the things we are turning our backs on are evil, but we wish to experience the difference between wanting and physical need. Fasting for 24 hours is a great experience. Noticing how the mind creates stories to persuade you to eat. Yes, it is challenging, but with tenacity we can remain mindful and study the working of the mind during this 24-hour period, to see how it is chatting to us and making the physical need something more.

All the time, we approach this practice with a sense of gentleness. The Buddha worked with deepest compassion with his disciples. Never judging, he was always seeing the suffering in them, understanding its root and having the deepest desire to help to free them from that suffering. We can do this too, with ourselves. We can step back from ourselves, from our own internal mental objects. We can find our own Buddha-nature, a genuine caring for ourselves, seeing our wish to make spiritual progress, to develop compassion and to see what makes us suffer. We watch our own mental processes with gentle compassion, maybe a feeling of fond amusement because this is what the mind does. It craves and it embellishes the craving. We don't hate it for doing this. We love it, but gently turn from it, looking behind it, to see what is there. What can I find behind my mind?

This nature of craving arises a great deal in meditation. Therefore, it gives us a lot of opportunity for gentle, safe practice, to investigate, to enquire.

We can work with the body scan (see 5.3) to notice even in an early part of the meditation, the mind is wanting to move on, to other areas of the body, reaching out for something more interesting to do. We can notice this behaviour with gentleness and fondness and come back to wherever we got to. We seek to notice this mental behaviour earlier and earlier, when it is just the seed of a craving emerging in the mind.

Then when we move on to the breath, we focus on the anapana spot, that point just at the entry point of the nose, just feeling the sensation of the breath as it comes and goes - just the sensation of the breath. Again, we experience the nature of craving. The mind, looking to occupy itself with other things, nurturing the ego.

7.6   The sound of silence

Over the years I have found this meditation approach one of the most powerful for my spiritual progress and understanding. It is the meditation that I keep coming back to. I use it regularly, combining it with the meditation on the breath.

The Magic of Noticing – Andy Spragg

So, what is it? I came to it practising at Amaravati monastery, in Hertfordshire, one weekend. Ajahn Sumedho, the abbot of the monastery back then was leading the meditation and introduced us all to the sound of silence. I heard it almost immediately and realised that I had been hearing it all my life and hadn't noticed. There it was, hiding in plain sight. It was so surprising I nearly fell off my cushion.

The sound of silence is known in many cultures. A whole yogic system was developed around it called Nada Yoga. It is known in South America and here the Incas attached great significance to it, believing it originated from the gods. There are many theories about where it comes from. It could be the resonance of the human mind, the echo of the birth of the universe. Some have even said that it is the voices of long dead ancestors.

For me, having listened to it for many years, I think it could be the resonance of the brain as it seems to manifest inside the head. Alternatively, the cosmic hum could also be true.

Actually, I do not believe that what it is matters. In practising we should let go of all our preconceptions of what it might be. Notice perhaps if your natural inclination is to find some deep spiritual meaning in the sound. Let that go. That preconception will, itself, get in the way of the practise. The sound is just the sound. Accept it and go into it.

How can we have a sound of silence? It is very much akin to space. When we enter a room, we focus on the objects. We do not necessarily notice the space between the objects. But the space is just as important. At Amaravati, Ajahn Sumedho asked us to just spend a moment, sitting on our cushion and cast our eyes around in that lovely shrine room. The shrine room at Amaravati is a beautiful space, very simple and unadorned. But somehow it is the big beautiful space that makes it so spiritual. It does not need lots of wall hangings or vibrant colour. The space is special. And so it is with sound. Because sitting behind all sounds, we find the sound of silence. There is never complete silence, because it is always there.

It sounds a little like white noise. When you pick it up it has within it a whole range of frequencies. It is not a single frequency like a bell. It has thousands of frequencies within it. It varies and changes constantly both in pitch and volume. It is far from static. Step into a silent space and you will hear it. And of course, just like the breath, it is always with us. So, like the breath, we can use it to anchor ourselves when life is kicking off. The more you practise with it, the more apparent it will be. When Ajahn Sumedho described it to us he said that he had been meditating by a waterfall once and heard it sitting under the sound of the thundering water. At the time, all those years ago, I found this a challenging concept. Some years later, I was riding my motorbike through the middle of a busy town. I pulled up at some lights and heard it. Despite the grumble of the bike's engine and the traffic around me, I could hear it.

When we go into the sound of silence it can teach us many things. Firstly, notice if you have a resistance to it. Maybe you are focussing on other sounds that are more usual. You hear them because, like the objects in the room, they demand your attention.

The Magic of Noticing – Andy Spragg

But just as we can start to notice the space in the room, we can move our attention away from the more obvious sounds and listen to the constant sound behind them.

When the other sounds distract you, the sound of silence is particularly powerful at developing concentration. We have to relax into it. We don't see space unless we look beyond the objects.

Interestingly, the more we drop into the meditative state, the louder the sound becomes. Again, coming back to the idea of space, when we first moved into the Shrine room at Amaravati, did not see space. I saw cushions, monks, pillars and the shrine. I took Ajahn Sumedho's direction to help me see the space and this was when I was settled, relaxed and easing into a meditative state.

It is the nature of this meditation that helps us move into the gentle state of Samadhi, that soft gentle single pointed concentration. The sound of silence is especially conducive to this. I have found that it is a very powerful way to move up through the levels of absorption in meditation.

The Sound of Silence can be used to access this tricky concept of no-self. By letting go of self, we learn to connect more deeply with the world around us. As we connect more deeply, we let go of self more and more - a spiral effect. So the sound of silence is an incredible way to explore this. In order to hear it, we seem to have to really connect with space. With the world outside of us. But because we don't "hear" it in the traditional sense, it is more our mind that is connecting with the space around us rather than our traditional senses. So, you really get a feeling of softening the

The Magic of Noticing – Andy Spragg

boundary between self and the world. The more that boundary softens, the more we hear the sound.

7.7 Empty your cup - The art of contemplation

The more I practise, the more I see the value of the old Zen story of the master filling the student's teacup. The master keeps pouring and pretty soon the teacup overflows. But he keeps pouring and the student cries out to him. The master explains that the student needs to first empty his cup.

Buddhist practice is not dogmatic in its approach. Yes, it has those things that sit in the background that we are challenged with understanding – "no self", for example.

But, as a practising Buddhist, we are taught to practise, not taught to learn. This is interesting. Although we have the guidance of the Pali canon containing the sutras guiding us, we do not learn them by rote. We practise with their guidance.

For example, have you ever built an Ikea wardrobe? Because the instructions are so good it is a relatively easy task. The first wardrobe I ever built was from MFI and the instructions were terrible! So, I had to practise. I would construct a part of the wardrobe, working my way through the instructions and discovering bit by bit what was meant by the very unclear instructions. There were lots of retries and a few big "aha" moments along the way, when the penny dropped on what the instructions were trying to tell me.

The Magic of Noticing – Andy Spragg

For me, Buddhist practice feels a little like this. The instructions are a little vague; they do not entirely fit in with the context of this modern world, but in places there are very detailed explanations for approaches.

The sutras tell us about the four noble truths and explain that life is suffering. That suffering and the understanding of what leads to suffering, allows us to move towards true understanding and enlightenment. I think in ancient India life would have been much harder and therefore the suffering was probably more obvious. In this modern world with all our wealth, the newcomer finds it difficult to see this suffering, particularly if they come from a privileged background.

But then, the Satipathana sutra goes into great depth about mindfulness and the practice of meditation, setting out detail around practices like anapanasati, mindfulness of breathing.

The approach I suggest taking here is contemplation. Normally I recommend not thinking, just feeling. However, with contemplation, here we apply creative thought to take us forwards. We do have this tool after all, so let us use it. But we do not approach the contemplation in an academic way.

Instead, I recommend applying that same feeling and experiencing process. When I built that wardrobe, even if I had learnt the instructions off by heart, it would not have allowed me to build the wardrobe any quicker. In fact, if I had stuck to the instructions, I would have finished up with a mis-shaped pile of MDF instead of a wardrobe. The same applies here, I believe. We should take the texts and see how they work with our life. We can understand something about the end product, so we look at how the instructions might apply to our world.

Some of the concepts are very difficult. I mentioned earlier about Tibetan cosmology. But we do not have to believe in these realms on a universal scale. We can equate this, to our life. We can look at how these different realms appear in different people and even inside ourselves at different times of the day.

- Realm of the gods
- Realm of the demi-gods
- Realm of the human
- Realm of animals
- Realm of hungry ghosts
- Realm of hell

Here, the human realm is considered to be the most likely place where we can enter into enlightenment. In all the other realms, a mindful existence is very difficult.

We can weave this into another sutra and see how this can transpire - the Bahiya sutra. Here we hear the very clear description of using the pure senses to stay fully present and mindful. The Buddha tells Bahiya, "the seen will merely be the seen, the heard will merely be the heard, the sensed will merely be the sensed".

Of course, we understand this as remaining mindful and present and attempting to not let the ego invade our experience, i.e., the veil of our selves.

The Magic of Noticing – Andy Spragg

We can contemplate how this sutra comes into our daily lives. Here we are sitting squarely in the human realm, feeling calm and mindful. Then we finish our practice and head out to our car where we find the tyres have been slashed. Our contemplation can then consider how we react to this. Certainly, something more than just seeing and merely seeing will occur. The sutra expresses that the cognised will merely be the cognised. Of course, we feel anger bubble up. But if we contemplate this, we can see that we can accept and understand the anger and not feel guilty about it later. Provided we do see the anger, feel it, notice it, accept it and do not allow it to control us. The knowing or awareness of anger is not anger itself. We learn through mindfulness and contemplation. Otherwise, we certainly will move away from the human realm and slip into one of the others!

So, my advice here is, do not get hung up on what you believe in. Think about what you can reflect on and see how it comes into your own life. Even difficult concepts like rebirth and the absence of self, we can bring into our own existence. We do not have to see them strictly as physical truths. In this way, we empty our cup. Or better still, we see that it was never full in the first place. The stuff we thought was in our cup is not really there.

But in order to lead a contemplative approach in this way we need a settled mind first. The more settled and calm the mind is, the more space for acceptance and understanding. We will not be so judgemental towards ourselves, and we will not slip away from the awareness and get caught into the loop of our emotions and their triggered actions.

First, we need to develop that empty cup - mindfulness of breathing. Then, we can experience the essence of the Bahiya sutra through passive listening and the sound of silence.

7.8   Overload

These days we seem to have lots of new words creeping into our language and certainly in the recent year or two many of them are not too positive in terms of our modern lifestyle.

Two that are coming up more often these days are overload and burnout. Both are essentially making a critique of our lifestyle today.

We seem to have forgotten how to take care of ourselves and others. Many of us are working ourselves into the floor and our news services certainly do not help.

Overload and Burnout - of these two words, I think they are to a degree, chronological in nature. Overload comes first, followed by burnout.

Which is why, here I focus on overload. In many ways, if we have reached a point of burnout, all we can really do is stop everything. Stop work, rest and recuperate. Because if we do not, then the next step after this is illness. Both burnout and overload are mental symptoms. It if we don't find a way to step back from these then, for sure, physical Illness will come next.

So, overload is a very good place to start.

Even in overload, we will feel a physical manifestation. When we are stressed, we very much feel it in our bodies. Our bones ache.

So, we need to develop a habit of paying attention to our bodies not in a superficial way but in a very deep way. Even down to the cellular level, if you like. Sound impossible? Well it isn't. Even in the early days of meditation we detect fine tingling sensations on the surface of the skin. Even then, we have taken our concentrated awareness down to a much greater depth than we are normally in.

This is why, in Buddhist meditation we often start with the body scan because it draws us into the body. When we are in meditation, we are essentially in a very protected, nurturing environment, so we bring the full focus of our mind to developing habit. The habit we develop initially is the awareness of the body and particularly for identifying tension in the body. Tension manifests whenever any type of stress is present, and it appears both in the mind and in the body. We can only do something about tension if we notice it. Then we can bring the mind to bear and let go of the tension. This is the starting point - to find tension in our internal experience and learn to let it go.

Clearly with overload there are certain things we should do to lesson then load. To-do lists can help but only note down three or four top must dos. Having a long list of to-dos can make us feel even worse. Then we need to do what is known as swallow the frog. A horrible phrase, but it is a very healthy practice. Each day figure out which item on your list you are avoiding and DO IT. Swallow the frog.

But overload doesn't just happen because we have a long to-do list. If there is lots of worry in the family, bad stuff in the news, fears and worry about the future this all contributes. Again, there are some more mundane things we can do, like coming away from the news and social media.

But here we can also use meditation. Just as we can recognise tension in the body and let go, we can also do this with the mind. But we must not think this is about the thoughts that are flowing through the mind; certainly not. Here we are talking about Mind itself. How does your mind feel?

The more we practice with meditation the more we start to feel this. Then we become aware that our mind almost feels like a muscle and we can relax it.

Just for a moment, take your awareness into the front area of your head, inside your head. See what you can feel. Now, picture a compassionate gaze behind the eyes, as if you are looking at something or someone you love. Now notice that feeling in that part of the head. When we do this, we often feel a "loosening" in the area, like our brain is letting go.

7.9   The practise of the unborn self

There is a simple practise we can do. We can first give ourselves a simple little Mantra. "I am Andy, I am Andy..." over and over again. (Obviously, use your own name, not mine!!) Do this for five minutes or so. Then, simply stop and sit. You will immediately notice a sense of peace and quiet and a sense of relief. Running through that mantra for five minutes is hard work. Also, you find that the mind starts pondering the questions that the mantra invokes. Sometimes, it becomes a question all of its own "Am I Andy?"

The Magic of Noticing – Andy Spragg

The other big thing we notice is that when we stop, we become aware of the present moment through our five senses. There is nothing else going on. We tune in to our bodies, to sounds, and just sit.

This is very much the practice of the unborn self. When we are physically born, do you think the ego is born as well? Or does it get developed through our formative years? The age-old question of nature versus nurture arises here. I certainly do not think the entirety of the ego is present at physical birth, even if some element of it is present. I believe that we are pretty much a blank canvas. There will be some character traits that are genetic, but the main bulk of our mental habits are laid down during our formative years. Hence the name, the formative years. Actually, it doesn't matter at what age the term formative years applies to. It may be different for different people. But key here is that at our physical birth, in terms of ego, there is not much there. A new-born is simply aware and soaking up their surroundings directly. They are not interpreting very much at all, because they have no experience to base their interpretation on. They are little Buddhas! Or are they? Well they have the capacity for pure awareness, that is certainly true, but they do not have the cognitive ability yet to direct themselves in the way an adult does. They cannot yet direct their compassion or choose the skilful path.

At this stage in life, a baby will no doubt experience compassion when it gazes at its parents, but it won't be able to focus it with intent in a given situation. Also, even awareness at this stage is the random open awareness (that we all have and use all the time) not the calm concentrated awareness of Samadhi. Dogs are like this too. They live in the moment, beaming up at their owners with compassion and driven by continuous distraction from the world around them. They do live in the moment, very much so. But they don't have the ability to focus themselves the way we do.

So, our challenge is to get back to that simplified state of the new-born infant but with the ability to bring a calm concentrated awareness to our experience and focussed and full compassion into our lives. This is why we meditate.

So, what do I mean by the unborn self? Put simply, it is the self that was not born. The self that perpetuates through our lives, the self that we often falsely see as being somehow permanent and unchanging. It is the self that we invest a huge amount of our energy in protecting. It is the self that causes us suffering when we misinterpret a friend's comment as a slight against us and get angry. When we are mindful during our day, we can pay attention to our thoughts as they arise and ask ourselves, how many of them come from a place of protecting the ego?

I must just correct a common misconception. As a Buddhist, I do not believe having an ego is a bad thing. The ego is not evil! But in order for us to truly make spiritual progress we have to connect with the world exactly as it is and accept it the way it is and what stops us from doing that is the ego. So, it gets in the way. This is why, thoughts driven by the ego tend to often produce suffering in some way, shape or form, whereas thoughts driven from pure awareness tend to take us forward. They are driven by wisdom.

The Magic of Noticing – Andy Spragg

So, how can we investigate this in meditation? The best way is to just experience it, and, in my practice, I have found the sound of silence is perfect for this.

7.10 Embracing Change. Journeying through from fear and disquiet to stillness and tranquillity

Change is inevitable. We hear that phrase so often and many little sayings pop up on my Facebook feed featuring this phrase. But just reading the words doesn't really help.

We have a great opportunity to practice with change in our lives. The years 2020 and 2021 really demonstrated this to us when the COVID-19 pandemic arrived, and we worked our way through, moving into lockdown and then back out.

Inevitably we feel that change pulling on us, and this can manifest as fear and anxiety. Even in our more confident moments we perhaps feel a level of disquiet.

In order to accept something and let it go, we have to take hold of it first. To let go of a ball, we have to have it in our hand first.

The same applies here. It is certainly true that change is inevitable. We can't escape it. In fact, a little later in this section we will turn this in to a positive. But first, if change is inevitable, we can't get rid of it. So, the only thing we can work on is the fear and anxiety itself. In other words, as the Buddha taught, it is not the change that causes our suffering, it is our reaction to that change.

The Magic of Noticing – Andy Spragg

All emotions appear in the body. The mind does the thinking, the body does the feeling. So, our first step is to get in touch with this aspect of our experience - the energetic quality of the emotion. How it feels in the body.

In the body scan meditation, we have touched this emotional side of experience, when we focus on the heart space and experience the raw nature of emotional feeling in the body. We should keep that practice present as often as we can, so that our watching and noticing state becomes habitual, staying steadily mindful of our body and keeping vigilant for emotional tension. When it arises, we focus on stepping into it with gentle softness and friendship, physically releasing that emotional tension.

But we have not fully grabbed it yet. We now feel the effect of change on the physical being, but we need to take a look at change itself. We need to see that nothing is static, and we need to experience this directly. Where can we experience this change directly? In a safe place to explore its nature? Back in the body. When we explore the body and our direct, honest experience of it, all we find is constant change, constant movement. Nothing is static. If the body is static for a long period of time we start to suffer with our health.

So, if change is inevitable, the natural order of things if you like, why do we suffer with it? If static is unnatural, wouldn't we fear a place where nothing changes? But we don't. We look for that and fear the other - strange! Buddhist thinking says that this occurs because of Mind. The thinking mind. This mind has an ego: a sense of self. This sense of self is not representative of the way the world actually is. It creates a picture of a sense of separation from the universe. There is "I" and there is everything else. This sense of seeks to constantly protect itself from perceived risk. Threats to i come from our desires and aversions. These external influence either feed our ego and make it feel safe and nourished or they threaten the ego and make it feel fear and diminished in nature So, our ego, or our thinking mind, responds by wanting to wrap itself with a view of a static world which does not change. We know the challenges are out there affecting us. If we can keep everything static, then perhaps we can keep ourselves free from the emotional reactions that come with those challenges. But through meditation having experience change and it inevitability, we have directly felt that it is impossible to keep everything static. Even our body, where you would think we would have direct control, is impossible to keep static. We canno stop change.

The only way to find that stillness and tranquillity we seek is to step away from Mind. To get in touch with the gardener, that par of the mind which sits and watches everything. This awareness i there all the time and has the capability of watching everything a work, seeing the thinking mind as it struggles to protect itself, a it strives to resist change and triggers the emotional turmoil in the body.

Through mind watching and stillness, using the breath to establish focus and gentle mind watching to notice when the ego interferes and strives to protect itself, we experience all three elements of this incredible process with gentle tenderness and friendship. After all this is all very human.

The Magic of Noticing – Andy Spragg

Gently, with practice, we are establishing a habit of noticing all this ego protection that goes on and slowly we allow ourselves to let go of this.

7.11 Patience

Life requires a huge amount of patience. Just think back through your own life and see all the moments when you had to be patient.

The Buddhist word for this, in Sanskrit, is Kshanti. This is generally translated as "patience", but it can also be translated as "forbearance", "endurance" and "tolerance".

However, it carries with it a sense of gentleness towards oneself. So, it doesn't involve the type of patience where we are gritting our teeth, harming ourselves, bottling up rage, or being a passive victim. When we are patient, in this sense of the word, we are taking care of ourselves. Sometimes we take care of ourselves by being patient. I think we can all agree that most of the time, if not all the time, impatience kind of adds more problems to situations.

Kshanti is a form of awareness, an awareness of suffering in which one does not react with anger. Key here is the awareness of suffering. If we can see suffering in a situation, then this becomes the prerequisite for us to be able to be patient. By way of example, if we can perhaps start to see somebody who annoys us as suffering in some way, and acknowledge our responsibility in that dynamic that's going on between us and this other person, then we start to let go of the annoyance. It is not really about excusing them. If they acted unethically in some way, then it is more than justified that we push back, but also, if we can see and understand their suffering in the situation, we can then develop a degree of patience with them and perhaps act more skilfully ourselves.

The Dhammapada says, "Patience is the highest austerity." At the time of the Buddha and even today in India there are all kinds of people who are going around trying to purify themselves and practice spiritually by acts of self-mortification: starvation, holding your arm up for six months until it starts to wither away, this kind of thing. Interestingly this kind of idea, maybe in more subtle forms, still exists today. I think actually many of us approach our jobs in this way, seeing it as some form of self-sacrifice. Throwing ourselves in too deep, burning ourselves out and not seeing that this is an unwholesome practice. But the Buddha said, "you do not need to physically harm yourself." In other words, you do not need to go out looking for trouble; trouble will find you, because our world is absolutely full of opportunities for us to practise patience. So, "patience is the highest austerity."

To explore patience, we can explore the difference between patience and impatience. There is a Taoist saying, "Soft overcomes hard," or "Soft wisdom overcomes hard wisdom." And, by hardness I mean resistance, being brittle or rigid. These are not wholesome mental states. Many of us find that our response to stress or some kind of challenge is that we tend to develop a protective tenseness, or a kind of toughness. This is therefore where we can work. We work on the physical thing first. We just learn to soften.

In this way, we keep the energy flowing between us and the world, even when we momentarily might hate the world sometimes. As we become mindful, we notice our relationship with patience.

The Magic of Noticing – Andy Spragg

Some people are very patient with other people, but they'll get really annoyed if they lose their keys, or if the toothpaste tube isn't working, or the PC is running slow (that's me, by the way). Some people have a lot of patience for animals and children, but hardly any for adults. All of these are excellent places for us all to start practising! Starting with the easier steps is a good idea. That way we can have some practice for when more challenging things come around.

We can look here at four steps we can work through for developing a practice of patience.

7.11.1 Rationalisation

Through meditation and mindfulness, we start to notice and work on our self-justifications for our lack of patience, and we start to see the truth, or rather the lack of truth in those justifications. These self-justifications appear as dialogue in the mind. Mindfulness reveals that dialogue to us and when we hear what it is saying, we notice how if it is justifying how we are feeling. Then we notice, of course, that those justifications are not valid, accurate or wholesome.

Especially anger or other unskilful mental states. For example, righteous indignation. This is us telling ourselves that our anger is good, justifying our feelings. Anger is never good. Definitely human, but not wholesome.

Why do we always need to tell ourselves that we are right, or that we are wrong, or that we are good, or that we are bad? Doing this just puts another veil between us and what we are trying to perceive. It is a source of our suffering. Some people might argue that it is suffering to tell yourself you are bad, but it is not suffering to tell yourself you are good. Although one might be slightly preferable over the other, I think they are both not necessarily telling us the truth, especially if they are supporting us rationalizing negative mental states. So, we have anger. There is nothing wrong with anger insofar as it is just energy, just energy coming out, bursting forth even. But, when we are talking about expressing it, we need to be very careful, or at least mindful, about what we are doing. We need to not harm ourselves and other people, and this can be very tricky, because we do not want to repress or swallow the feelings and we certainly do not want to cause harm.

This is why just being aware of our thoughts and emotions is so important, especially when they are strong. As we start to become mindful and notice how we react to strong emotion we notice how we pin the emotion on somebody else as blame. We start to understand that the emotion is born out of our ego and its desire to nourish and protect itself. When we notice this and let go, then, quite naturally, patience emerges.

7.11.2 Expectations: dealing with the realities of life

This is a complex world we live in and create around us, full of systems and process. No kind of system is going to be perfect, and it is guaranteed that some of the time it will break down. That is just the way things work. If we cannot cope with these times when our systems break and force us to change plans suffering of course comes in and this manifests as fear or anger.

For example, one thing that is not an accident is illness, or physical pain. Illness is an intrinsic part of the human form, and no one on

The Magic of Noticing – Andy Spragg

Earth has ever escaped it. Yet, our expectations are such that we expect that we are not going to get sick. We also seem to have an innate resistance to ageing.

Many of these expectations are unconscious. Academically, we understand them but then, when they happen to us, we are surprised by them.

Age, the one thing that is perfectly obvious that it's going to happen, and yet, when it does, we find ourselves thinking "Wow, I didn't see that coming!"

The realities of life can be tough, but they are realities, so they are not going to go away. We always have to remember the Buddha's words here. We do not suffer because of these realities of life. We suffer because of how we react to them. Again, here, when the ideas or thoughts associated with any of these realities enter our minds, we experience emotion and tension in body and mind. So, we focus on this tension instead and soften into it. We meditate on the raw energy of the emotion and soften into this.

7.11.3 Defensiveness: using our soft spots as teaching tools
Or as John Kells, Tai Chi master, used to say, invest in loss. Much of what happens to us, happens at an unconscious level. In other words, our mind has reacted to something in the world and emotions and thoughts are being formed. But unless we are mindful in that moment, we simply do not notice. Perhaps, someone just says something, they themselves might not even think they are saying anything controversial, but our response to it is that we feel like we are being attacked. Somebody else could say exactly the same thing to someone else and it does not bother

The Magic of Noticing – Andy Spragg

them, but for some reason this person hits a spot for us. We migh not even know that we have that "spot" there. Somehow the comment is hitting our sense of vulnerability or our fragility.

Through the practice of mindfulness we become aware of these moments. Again, we have emotion and tension associated with this. We focus on the tension and the emotion instead of the "thing" we thought was upsetting us. We focus on our reaction not the thing itself. Maybe we can ease up on blaming other people a bit if we just realize that we are being defensive, which is not to say that our feelings are invalid (or anything like that), but it's something to be aware of. And if somebody else is being super touchy, maybe having a bit of sensitivity around that too, rathe than trying to be right, just seeing what we can do to connect with the situation.

7.11.3.1 Doormat (passivity): avoiding abuse by looking at our attitude
So, the last of these areas to examine when we are investigating this attitude of patience with our mindfulness practice is the doormat approach, and this could be called "Passivity".

If we think of the Dharma, the Buddha's teaching, as the pinnacle of sanity and health, we will realize that any form of abuse is certainly not going to be a part of it. It is really easy to see and recognise when others are suffering with abuse or some form of unwholesome behaviour, but it is much more difficult to see it in ourselves. When we perhaps feel that tension or emotion that arises out of such treatment, quite often our first reaction will be to blame ourselves for it. Co-dependence and patience are wha are called "near enemies" in Buddhism. In other words, we migh actually mistake one for the other. But they are not the same, a least in the motivation behind them, because co-dependence is motivated by fear, insecurity, confusion, craving, all sorts of other things. Patience is motivated by an understanding of how things are and understanding of interconnectedness that is infused with love. I have known couples where the wife is actually in a co-dependent relationship with an abusive husband. However badly he treats her, she seems to "put up with it" and self-heroically expresses this as her patience with him because she believes she loves him. This can, of course, work in any relationship dynamic.

So, rationalization, expectation, defensiveness, and doormat behaviour are areas we can bring mindfulness into. Also, more proactively, we can resolve to bring patience into a situation or to a person before we even see them. In this way it is a way to engage with the challenges of life. We don't know what's going to happen when we walk out the door. We don't know at any time what's going to happen, so in a way, we accept this unexpected nature of life, letting go of emotions and tensions associated with it. Because challenges will be there, and they will be unexpected. If we are going to truly avoid suffering, we work on changing our reaction to this nature of the world. The common ground, you may have seen with all four areas is that of focussing on the tension and the emotion that arises, rather than focussing on the problem. So, we develop a habit of noticing that tension. That will reveal which of these behaviours may be kicking in. Is our impatience with life emerging because we are –

1. Rationalising and self-justifying our negative states
2. Are our expectations of life unreal(istic)?
3. Are we acting defensively to things that don't exist?

The Magic of Noticing – Andy Spragg

4. Are we being passive to how we are being treated?

7.12 Disquiet

Disquiet is an agitated and troubled state and it is for this reason that it affects our meditation so much. It is sometimes translated as anxiety or worry but this really does not bring out the full breadth of the word. The Pali word Kaukrtya fuses the meaning of both these words.

Read any Buddhist text and it will teach us to constantly approach our meditation with a sense of gentleness towards ourselves. With this topic of disquiet, we certainly must do that. It is very easy when exploring disquiet to drop into self-judgement and self-recrimination.

Disquiet is extremely persistent. It lurks. All disquiet must be investigated by us if we are to make progress. It cannot be suppressed. It will simply lurk in the shadows and hinder our progress in meditation. When suppressed it becomes cynicism, sloth, depression, self-hatred and the blaming of others.

In terms of ethics, it can come from a place that is either driven by skilful or unskilful behaviour in some way or it can be ethically neutral, and we will see why with some examples. In terms of its effect on us (from a Karmic perspective) it can also be wholesome or unwholesome. This is sometimes surprising. But when we see how disquiet can result in the blaming of others we begin to understand why.

Let us take an example of its wholesome form. Imagine that you have just had a heated exchange with somebody. Afterwards, you feel a nagging unease. This is something more than just the unpleasant after-effects of the other person's rudeness. Thinking it over, you discover that the source of the nag is when you admit to yourself that you spoke harshly or not quite truthfully. You realise that this is the source of your discomfort. We often push away such feelings, but this type of introspection is wholesome. It has enabled you to see, with clarity, the true nature of the situation and your part in it. It then of course gives you the opportunity to take some action and put the situation right! Here the mere act of investigating and understanding the feelings coming out of the exchange is karma and the karma vipaka (the result) that arises, is understanding. Already you have changed your situation and moved forward.

We can of course then take things further and reflect on the aspects of our character and ingrained mental behaviour that make us act the way we do in the exchange. What are we holding on to or what are we resisting? Not in terms of the practical object of the discussion but in the general sense of you as a person and the way you react to things in given situations. When we conduct this type of introspection and investigation during our meditation, we must stay away from the story behind the exchange itself and see the general patterns of our behaviour. This way we start to smooth out those ruts in the road - our ingrained mental habit.

In a way, this process is like the confessional, although no one else is involved. In order to make progress we must approach it with brutal and total self honesty, but always balanced with a sense of gentleness towards our self. The power of remorse is directly proportional to our spiritual aspiration. Not guilt, we must understand, but remorse. The two are different. Guilt burns us out from the ground up. Remorse is a positive process and we should see it as that. When we find aspects of ingrained habit we should celebrate. We have uncovered something, and we can therefore do something about it. This is extremely positive.

However, what I have found in my own practice is that we can also have false disquiet. The previous example is true disquiet, i.e., we have behaved in a way which we should look at and explore through remorse. But there are types of disquiet which arise where we have no reason for remorse. But disquiet still arises. For example, the withdrawal of someone's love or the rejection by a group, work colleague etc. These are quite often hard ingrained patterns of mental behaviour that were established during childhood. Not being invited to a friend's party when we know that all our other friends are going. Not being picked for the sports team perhaps. These types of event make a big impression when we are young and stay with us. These mental behaviours play in and they can cause complications. For example, false disquiet can play into truly moral or ethical situations. This sometimes happens when we truly have done something wrong, but the disquiet is coming from a fear of punishment rather than the real empathetic concern for those we have hurt.

In our modern world, interestingly, the focus is more on the false disquiet. We are encouraged to pay more attention to the false disquiet, to the prospect of punishment. What a different place the world would be if we all focussed on true empathy instead? But actually, if we do not look this in the eye, understand where we need to make change and work, we can potentially end up in a place of insecurity or potentially neurosis.

Then there is a third angle that I have found in the exploration of this area. This is called functional disquiet. This does not have any moral dimension at all. It happens just because of our fallible human selves. Have you ever left the house for the day and wondered if you actually locked it properly? You spend the whole day with that nagging worry. Functional disquiet is very useful. It helps us and protects us but if we let it, it can develop into anxiety or full-blown OCD conditions.

So, we have the three forms of disquiet; ethical, false and functional. The knowing and the watching of these areas of our mental habit give us a vehicle to examine some of the murkier areas of our emotional life and start to lift the lid a little.

Some of this may take some effort and time. We need to detangle behaviours which are definitely unskilful from those which are perhaps ingrained through old prejudices, aggressive and blame based belief systems (which clearly are false in their nature) and our habits which exhibit themselves as anxiety-based thinking.

We do need to truly feel this kind of experience to progress but by seeing it we do not let it control us. We can use our own disquiet as our meditation subject!

So, in meditation we can sit and look at our progress in the meditation and to see if the hindrance of disquiet is present. If so, to contemplate a little and see whether it is ethical, false or functional or perhaps all three.

7.13 Liking and loving

Life can be complex sometimes. Where does that complexity come from? Our minds of course. Whenever we are faced with conflicting opinions internally or with choices that we do not have clear drivers one way or the other, or situations where we cannot see the positive, we get tense. Our emotional side kicks in and this can manifest in all sorts of ways, such as fear, anger or frustration.

So, I thought I would illustrate this with one of the complexities we all experience from time to time - liking versus loving.

A simple question. Are there things which we can love but do not like? This is an important question as it is very similar to a Zen koan. It does not seem to have an obvious answer. To put it another way, do we have to like something in order to love it? These questions prompt an emotional response, first and foremost. The first response that comes up might well be "well of course not. You have to like first in order to love" but all of us can then sit back and think about this and see examples where this is not the case.

What this question reveals to us is the difference between these two human mental conditions.

They do have one thing in common, however, they are both human mental conditions. (There is of course a high probability that other animals do possess these mental conditions. However, am a human. Knowing how an elephant would debate these two questions, will not help me understand it. And besides, I don't speak elephant)

The Magic of Noticing – Andy Spragg

We can therefore say that without a mind present, these two mental conditions would not exist. No liking, no loving. These mental conditions require mind to exist. A mind is present, perceiving something and liking or loving or even both arise.

Let's take a look at these two mental states and think about their effect on us. If we think about a vector of experience. At the one end of the vector we have pleasant and at the other we have unpleasant. Experiences touch our senses and the nature of these appear somewhere along this vector. We either like, or dislike or we feel relatively neutral about them. So, this mental state is about sensual pleasure in some way. We like things because they give us sensual pleasure in some way, shape or form. With obvious things like a nice smell or something pleasing to the eye, this process is easy to understand. But in Buddhist psychology we see six senses. Taste, touch, seeing, hearing, smelling and MIND. The mind is a sense organ just the same as the others. It is triggered by stimuli in just the same was as, say, the nose. A chemical enters the nose and triggers it. A thought enters the mind and triggers it. Both produce the same result. Like, dislike or neutral. Pleasant or unpleasant. So even mental objects like thoughts or memories produce a sensual response of like or dislike. If our mindfulness is strong, we can step back from the picture and see this happening in us.

So, what about loving. This one is really tricky. I wouldn't mind betting we can all think of things that sit on the unpleasant end of that vector, but we still love them. The most complex form of this appears when we think of other people. There are many examples where mothers, whose sons have gone off the rails and ended up as hardened criminals, still love them. The crimes they have

The Magic of Noticing – Andy Spragg

committed are violent. Inevitably their mothers won't "like" them very much, but they will still love them.

It is not so difficult to picture the person who cannot swim and fears the water, still stands on the beach and looks at the beauty of the sea, feeling a deep love for the view.

What does this mean for us and how does it help us? There are many things in life that cause us internal conflict and perhaps this is one of them. Maybe there are people or beings in the world where we perceive the beauty and others around us are expressing their dislike. If we look into the situation, we will probably discover the difference between like and love and the wisdom of understanding that difference will come through.

Social media is a terrible place for prejudice and judgement. A simple sentence gets placed on a post and the vitriol and judgement that comes back can be awful. Potentially there is the assumption that the poster somehow supports or "likes" what they have posted about. But we all need to be very careful here. We all have a very strong pre-disposition driven by our own biases. We all have a very different view of the things we like and the things we do not. Judging someone else for their likes and dislikes is rather irrelevant to us and does not really take us forward, especially as we will not understand what is driving the other person's views, and can only guess. Judging someone else never takes our personal spiritual practice forward. But maybe if we were brutally honest with ourselves, we may find we are getting some form of satisfaction out of the process of judging. We "like" it!

Social media actually distances us. If we were having these conversations face to face, we would probably take the trouble of clarifying comments made and discover that some of the misunderstandings were driven by the difference between liking or loving. Compassion breeds tolerance.

Tolerance carries two sides to it. We can choose to focus on the positive side of tolerance. The negative side is a grudging "putting up" with things. But here, we can now think about giving ourselves permission to love things that we do not actually like. Sometimes, all we need is that permission. When we do this, a deeper form of tolerance develops, and this comes accompanied with connection. When we give ourselves this permission, we take away the conflict and what is left is love and compassion.

Then we come to self. This discussion, for me, really emphasises the difference between guilt and remorse. In Buddhism, we see guilt as an unskilful but remorse as skilful. For a while, I struggled with this and could not really see the difference. I now think the difference comes out of this very discussion.

If we believe that love is the same as like, then when we do something wrong and contemplate ourselves, guilt arises. But if we can see and feel the difference, then we can dislike what we have done but still allow love for ourselves to come through. Remorse manifests. We see the error of our ways but also see the capability to fix it and, even more, to learn from it and go beyond it.

Chapter 8. Formal Buddhist thinking

In this section we look at some of the formal teachings directly from Buddhist practice. The Buddha gave us an excellent framework of advice to follow. None of this should be seen as formal doctrine. The Buddha encouraged us to investigate all these concepts ourselves. Buddhism is not a faith-based religion in that sense. It is an approach to investigate ourselves and the world around us and see the true nature of both.

8.1   Mindfulness

This term mindfulness is becoming more and more common in our language these days. However, there are many incorrect perceptions of it and probably a few outright myths. So, before we delve too deeply into the practice itself, I would like to set out what it is and what it is not.

You can think of mindfulness as a mind state. All of our mind states are the net result of something that occurs in our lives. Joy, fear, anger, love, calmness, agitation - all of these occur in us because of something that happens. Mindfulness is a very special state that sits around, between and above all of these other states.

There are some basic mind states that we all have. These are arranged into two pairs.

Firstly, the mind can be calm and concentrated, or it can be distracted, busy and agitated. All of us at any one time or other sit somewhere on the line between these two states.

Then we have the twin states of cerebral thinking and logical versus open minded, creative, outward looking, perhaps even religious openness. Again, we all sit to an extent between these two states. So, we can see these as twin vertices that our mind is sitting somewhere on, at any point in time. All of us will veer towards one or the other but any of us can occupy a different point along these vertices at any point of time, depending on what is going on in our lives. Mindfulness is a state which has the potential to be always present and can sit outside of these. It is capable of sitting and seeing what is going on. So, our lives may be dishing out turmoil to us which result in fear and disquiet, and we will find our mind state then will be agitated. Depending on the problem it may slip either towards the cerebral/logical, if we are trying to think through a problem or it may slip towards the more open, potentially religious state, if we are feeling powerless.

Just think back for a moment to an episode where you were stressed or anxious. Remember how that felt. Just recreate it in your mind for a moment. Now ask yourself where you were on those vertices? Clearly the mind was in an agitated state but what about those other vertices? Were you gnawing at the problem, like a dog with a bone, going over and over potential solutions, but not really getting anywhere, replaying what had happened or what you thought was going to happen? Or were you feeling adrift, powerless, frozen to do anything? Waiting for something or someone to come and rescue you.

We are all here on these vertices, all the time. Blown by the winds of the life.

The Magic of Noticing – Andy Spragg

Mindfulness is very special because it is the one quiet place that i always available to us, no matter what is going on. With practice it is a place we can always go to.

Because of this, I would like to dispel a myth that is commonplace Often mindfulness is portrayed as something we "do" to help u deal with stress or anxiety. Yes, it can help with these condition but mindfulness is there for us all the time. It is not a tool for fixin; mental health problems. If you are suffering with deep stress o anxiety, then this is mental trauma, and you need to see your G] and get some professional counselling, psychiatric support o hypnotherapy. Mindfulness is for all of us, all the time. It shoul be practised when we are feeling good in ourselves as well a when we are feeling not so good.

We do not train our bodies when we are suffering with an illness If we go out for a run when we have a streaming cold, it will no do us any good! So why do we think we should practise ou mindfulness when we are under stress or feeling anxious? Ou work on our physical body pays dividends if we approach it righ If we are fit, we are better placed to fight off illness. The same goe with the mind. If we practise and build strong mental reserve through mindfulness training, we will be better placed to handl the stresses of modern life.

So how do we do it? How do we develop the habit of mindfulness By meditation. Meditation is a safe place to practise as there i nothing going to happen to us. We are simply sitting on th cushion. We have put our busy life on hold, and we are devotin; our time to practise. What is meditation not? Well, it is not a sp therapy or something we just do at the end of our yoga practise

What may surprise you is that it is not something we do to find a moment of peace and tranquillity! That may arise from time to time but, more often than not, it does not. Meditation is simply watching, and primarily mind watching. We are paying attention to what is happening right now, in this moment, and that mostly includes what is happening in the mind.

One of the most common worries people have is that they cannot stop their minds thinking. Well, the truth is, you never will! It is what the mind does. Meditation is not about that. It is about stepping outside of the thoughts and letting them float through the mind without being drawn into them. It is about learning about and accepting the nature of mind.

To illustrate this, imagine you are at the cinema. Our cinema experience is very deep these days, designed to immerse us in the action that is happening on the screen. 3D and even 4D (movement and sensation) are now becoming common place, all designed to pull us further into the story. We literally lose ourselves in the film and with this, we are not aware of what is happening physically around us. But it is, of course, still there. The people are sitting next to us, the chair is under us and the pain in our right knee may be still there. When someone perhaps rustles a sweet packet behind us it pulls us back out of the movie, and we are aware again of our surroundings. Mindfulness and meditation are similar to this. The thoughts are flowing through the mind and we can allow ourselves to be drawn into them, just like the movie, or we can practise being fully present with our world around us.

Of course, there is a time for thinking, planning, analysing etc. Mindfulness allows us to focus the mind on what needs to be done, rather than getting distracted by all the other stuff that floats through. You will find, with mindfulness practice, that the mind is not an orderly place. The thoughts are chaotic and not necessarily relevant or related to your current task in hand.

You perhaps know someone whose conversations with you seem to fly around from one subject to another. Almost in the middle of a sentence they change tack and start talking about something else. Keeping up with the conversation in this case can be quite exhausting. With mindfulness practice we start to see how our own mind is constantly pulling us away. Our conversations naturally become more focussed, relevant, gentle, two way and, actually, compassionate. Of course, this affects the way we approach our work too.

Considering what is "unmindful" is probably a good way to explore what this mindfulness state is. However, we immediately need to be a bit careful here, that we do not bring judgement in towards ourselves or towards others. For example, we may feel that "unmindfulness is anything that anyone else keeps doing which I find particularly irritating". It is perfectly natural to think in this way – well, perfectly natural in a reactive sort of way – but it is not a very good starting point for a definition of mindfulness. We can very easily drop into the trap of being judgemental towards ourselves or others, even if we do not intend it. So, when thinking about the mindfulness, we need to step back and be mindful of our own thinking.

Rather than thinking about mindfulness as an aspect of our practice, in some academic sense, we must see it as a state. I suggest that we need to move away from thinking of mindfulness as a sort of separate practice – one among others. And I think we especially need to get away from thinking of mindfulness as something we can only give proper attention to occasionally, e.g., when we are on retreat. I have often found, when leading retreats, that it is not that easy to get people thinking in terms of overall mindfulness practice, rather than just their meditation. Remember, mindfulness is a state, not something we do.

When discussing mindfulness while of retreat, nine times out of ten – unless they are prompted – people will only talk about what is going on when they are sitting in the shrine room with their eyes closed. Obviously, we are all aware that mindfulness and meditation are not two separate things – we know that mindfulness in daily life comes out of our meditation, and feeds back into our meditation. But there does seem to be quite a widespread notion that the only way to practice mindfulness properly is to have some sort of special retreat space and everything has to be done really slowly. – like slow walking or mindful eating, We do, of course, have to learn and sometimes we have to ease this learning by giving ourselves the right conditions for practice. But here, I am explaining that mindfulness does not depend on this. We can be in a mindful state even when we are at work, in the midst of a hectic day

8.2   The worldly winds

We are constantly affected by external factors in our world and challenged by them. There are, of course, many millions out there in the world. Often, we focus on the things themselves, justifying their effect on us, particularly when it is a negative effect. In our world today this is heightened because of a move towards legal action for anything that goes wrong in life. Implying that we can always blame somebody else or something else. The implication is that we don't have to take responsibility for these things or acknowledge that they are actually a part of life. An implication that it is not right that challenge happens.

At the heart of the Buddha's teaching is the understanding of suffering. That suffering exists but there is a way to escape it by understanding its cause. As we understand, suffering arises not because of the things that happen to us, but because of our response to the things that happen to us.

We must learn to work on ourselves; to see how things out there are affecting us and to learn to accept the nature of life.

A vehicle to help us understand this is the worldly winds. These can be seen as pairs of opposites. We have

- Gain or Loss
- Pleasure or pain
- Fame or infamy
- Praise or blame

They are called the worldly winds because we are swept along by them. We can never just avoid them; they will catch us. So, we need to work to understand how we allow them to cause us suffering. This is good way to see this picture. Rather than believing that the challenge itself causes our suffering, we see how we are reacting to the challenge.

The Magic of Noticing – Andy Spragg

No matter how much wealth we have, these pairing will still touch us. So, if we continue to react to them in the same way, we will always suffer.

If we have an expectation that life will always be fair and pain-free, we will always suffer from the worldly winds. Our little irritations, sense of hurt or injustice, disappointments and grumbling pains in our body all reveal this underlying delusion. Learning to let go of our desires that sit underneath this is rather difficult. However, expecting the world to step up and satisfy all of our desires will be impossible. So, we are better to discover the deep peace of acceptance and letting go.

Of course, understanding how these winds affect us also shows us how we respond and, in that way, how we make our own impact on the world, bringing about the worldly winds for others. Because much of our response is habitual, this gets embedded as continuous mental habit depending on the wind that happens to be blowing at a particular point. This is karma. We will always mentally respond in a particular way when a particular wind is blowing. Then, of course this mental behaviour gets put into action.

Let us go into one or two of these pairings and take a look at how they drive us. Pleasure and pain are relatively obvious, as is gain and loss. So, let us take a look at praise and blame first. One of my teachers told me a story that he experienced with this one. Leading a retreat each morning he would lead the retreatants in a short mantra in the morning followed by a bow to the Buddha. At the end of the retreat one retreatant came up to him and said that she had been deeply moved by the mantra and the bow. It felt deeply spiritual. However, another retreatant came up and said that he had understood that Buddhism was not a religion and this behaviour had therefore disturbed him and spoiled the retreat. The monk was fascinated to feel the flip flop of emotions inside him.

Then we have fame and infamy. Interestingly social media really plays in to this. People getting seduced into thinking how wonderful it is that they have more than 400 friends on a particular platform without stopping to think how many of those they actually know! The fact that their friends will see that they have 400 "friends" makes them somehow feel positive, satisfied and even self-important. Of course, if they notice that just a single one of those people has "unfriended" them this can create an overreaction, even potentially leading to that other worldly wind loss.

The worldly winds, of course, do not always appear on their own. They sometimes intertwine creating a very complex feeling inside of us.

Buddhism teaches to approach the worldly winds through mindfulness. We set out what are essentially four steps.

1.   Recognise that they are there. This is simply the action of noticing the winds in our daily lives, noticing them arise and seeing our reactions to them. One traditional Buddhist approach is to see them as little demons touching our lives.

The Magic of Noticing – Andy Spragg

2.   Distinguishing control from influence. So here we look at what is actually happening. Yes, we can look at the situation and see if there is anything we can do to avoid the worldly wind but more often than not the event has happened, and we are simply left with the emotional response. Our ceiling fell down in our lounge some time ago. A definite experience of "loss"! But it was no good theorising about how we could have avoided this. The lounge would have looked very strange with props in it, holding up the ceiling. That ceiling was coming down eventually. Actually, it was rather lucky no one was in the room when it happened! When it fell, it didn't do it on purpose! So we can hardly blame the ceiling. But we could have let it wreck our weekend. We didn't. There was a rather large clean-up job to be done but gave us an excuse to crack on with the decorating.

3.   See the winds as opportunities. The winds are great teachers. They teach us grace, humility, patience, courage or whatever else the situation calls for. So, we can see them as opportunities to grow on our spiritual path. Hard as it is, we must learn to accept. Remember, no matter who we are or how rich we are, they will still touch our lives and cause us suffering if we allow them to do so. For each of the pairings, we can look at a particular learning. For gain and loss, the learning is generosity. If you are suffering with this worldly wind, look it in the eyes and find a way to apply generosity. For fame and infamy, just take a look at how deeply unique and individual you are, wonderful as you are, no need to be conforming to particular stereotypes. Apply the first stage of metta bhavana and offer yourself compassion. For praise and blame just look at truthfulness. See through the stories into what is actually happening. Try not to see sides, but see all sides at the

same time. Pleasure and pain can be tricky. We have to apply pure mindfulness here to see how desire and aversion are playing in, particularly with pain. We must soften into it and have a degree of acceptance about it. It is just another experience of life.

4.   Listen to our own stories that we tell. Often, when we are in the grip of the worldly winds, the emotions lead us to tell ourselves stories. Perhaps, for example, following some form of verbal attack (praise vs blame perhaps) we catch ourselves afterwards thinking of remarks or comebacks that we wished we had said in the heat of the moment. Instead, honestly ask yourself, "is this helping? Is this wholesome?" The answer will inevitably be no. Our own internal dialogue teaches us a great deal about the nature of our habitual mental processes. Step outside that dialogue and listen to it from the outside.

In meditation we can gently replay this moment, noticing its effect on our bodies and on our mental process. Then we use mindfulness to relax our bodies and our minds and see the internal dialogue that we have going on. In this way we learn to protect ourselves from our own reactions to moments such as these.

8.3   Five spiritual faculties

We can draw an analogy of the mind with the water bottle. The bottle forms a shape and when the water is poured in, it takes this state. Our minds are very similar. The container is the mind. But what are we pouring into it? I would suggest – awareness. We believe that awareness presents us with a pure view of the world. But actually, if we allow it, that view will take the shape of the container, in this case, our mind and its tone or mind-shape.

As an example, when you have a day which results in a stressed, busy, confused mind state, your thoughts will be very much like this. But when you are calm and relaxed, open and receptive your thoughts will be far reaching and creative.

Buddhist practice explores this aspect through the five spiritual faculties. They can be seen as vertices, with mindfulness in the middle.

They are —

Samadhi - Meditation/Concentration/Absorption
Vs
Virja - Energy/Enthusiasm/Interest

Sraddha - Faith/Confidence/Letting go
Vs
Prajna - Insight/Wisdom/Intelligence

So, we can look at our mind state and understand where we are sitting. We can view them as vertices along which we are sitting. We will have general, underlying tendencies which draws us one way or the other. Then the effect of our day will potentially change this for short periods of time. We can look at these states and see how they affect us and colour our view of the world. For example, if we are too drawn in by samadhi, we may find we are withdrawn and don't interact and connect very much with the people and the world around us. But if we are too drawn in by virja, we may find that our approach to the world is haphazard, chaotic and although we connect with people, perhaps we frustrate them because of our lack of focus.

Then if we come to the other axis, if we have too much sraddha, we may well feel like we can gain deep religious understanding, but it may well be misguided. We will have a tendency to follow whatever is said to us by teachers, without investigating for ourselves. The emotion of the moment carries us forward and we aren't even aware of this. Actually, in our sector of work, holistic therapy, you see many practitioners who exist in this state. They find it very difficult to see the value of the scientific methods of western medicine because it doesn't fit in with their mind state.

Conversely, if you have too much prajna, then you will tend to miss the spiritual and emotional side of experience. Again, with western medicine, we see examples of doctors who see no value in complimentary therapy. Recently, we have seen counselling and mental health funding move out of the NHS and into local council funding. This shows this type of behaviour reflected on the large scale.

Sati

Sitting in the middle we have the balanced state of Mindfulness. This is a knowing and acknowledgment of the influence of these different states directly on ourselves. It is pure self honesty. Now, it is VERY important to note that this is about looking at self, not looking at others. It is very easy to look at the examples we have just given and be critical. We can say to the doctor, "it's obvious that you need to consider the emotion and the energy in your treatment of a patient." BUT! That very criticism will inevitably be influenced by our own mind state, our own balance. So, if we are to truly make a difference, we must look at who we are and what our mind state is to the exclusion of all others. Who are we? What are we like? The Christian faith has a parallel here. In Matthew, Chapter 7 verse 5, Jesus says " you must remove the plank from your own eye, before you try to remove the speck from your brother's." On first view, this appears to be a very strong message against hypocrisy. But I believe it goes deeper, challenging us to look at all aspects of ourselves. The five spiritual faculties are a very good starting point.

I said at the start that our minds are the container, into which the fluid is poured. Now we can perhaps consider what the fluid is? In my own practice, I believe the fluid is pure awareness. A lot of my practice these days focusses on the nature of awareness. Asking "What is I?" In order to uncover the answer to this, I must strive to ensure that the container is as pure and undented as possible. How do we achieve this? Through practice of mindfulness. That un-judging, open, totally honest, bare attention state where we can sit and look, and see.

This we can explore in meditation. Through the mindfulness of breathing we must first take the lid off our container to allow awareness, in its purest form, in. Then, we develop the habit of mindfulness or mind watching by concentrating on the breath.

8.4   The seven factors of awakening

The Buddha laid down his teachings to help us develop our spiritual path.

In these teachings described the seven factors of awakening. Rather than a recommended path this is more a description of "what is". We can imagine a tree with seven branches. These are not static; they are all growing all the time. The same is true for these seven factors.

They are -

- Mindfulness
- Investigation (of phenomenon)
- Diligence
- Ease
- Joy
- Concentration
- Letting go

Let us take a look at these in turn because I believe they help us to establish a regular practice for meditation. For me, they have been an antidote to doubt, when it has arisen.

Mindfulness. When I contemplate mindfulness, I like to think of it in terms of pure awareness. But there is no "I" in this awareness. just get in the way and stop the ability to just see what i happening here and now. So here, as this branch develops on th tree, we start to move away from self and just see our own mind and the world around us more directly. We lift the veil.

In order for us to progress spiritually though, we can use that very human factor that is in all of us - that ability to investigate; th second factor of awakening. Developing an enquiring mind i healthy. But we must allow the first branch to contribute here. W do not investigate properly if we think we already know th answer. Everything, absolutely everything, every day, we mus approach with a view to freshly investigate. And of course, w direct our attention to the things that give us spiritual progress

Politics may provoke a great deal of thought, but I cannot do much about influencing it directly and it is not really going to take me forward on my spiritual journey. My relationship with others, however, will take me forward and I can certainly investigate this. In Tai Chi, another art I teach, we often looked at yielding and conflict. John Kells (Tai Chi Master), to whom I have already referred, used to say "invest in loss". This was not, for me, the most powerful way of putting it, but I understand it to mean that every time I have conflict in my life, there is an opportunity to practise. Conflict and how I respond to it is very worthy of investigation.

The third factor of awakening is energy, perseverance or diligence. For me, this one rather feeds off the others. The more we practise in this way, the more we understand. The more we understand, the more we want to understand and feel the results of our labours. It starts with some understanding of the miracle of our existence. For me, this is staring us in the face but for many people, it is hidden from view. We get so caught up in life. We worry about the mortgage, how our children are getting on at school, what's going to happen if we are made redundant, what happens if the car fails the MOT etc. We forget to notice the simple miracle that we can actually feel our feet touching the floor. Frankly, that is amazing. As a human being we can feel that. We are aware of it and that simple fact, if we pay enough attention to it, could potentially take us all the way to enlightenment. Walking meditation is a major part of Theravada practice. It should not be underestimated in terms of its benefits. So, we apply the energy in the places when it matters. In terms of the areas above, most of these are "waiting" things. So why waste energy on them? Instead, practise. Put your energy into mindfulness. Yes, there are certainly times where we have to apply thought. But if you actually look, with total self honesty, at your day. You discover how little control you actually have over it.

Ease. Stop doing and do more being! When I first came to this one, I didn't really understand what it meant. I was striving hard with meditation. I was discovering more and more but I was getting tired. And then, I hit a solid wall. Or rather a plateau. Months and months of meditation and not feeling like I was making progress. At this time, I was also doing a lot of running. This was me as a younger man. Lots of physical exercise, lots of tai chi, lots of meditation, thinking that all this was making a difference. I was also carrying a lot of pride with all. Then one day, while out for a run, I injured my calf muscle. I stopped running. No more running that day. I was halfway across a meadow. It was stunning. The sun was out, and the meadow was alive with life. I hadn't noticed the first half of the meadow. I was too busy running, pushing myself. Which is probably why I injured my calf muscle in the first place! When I stopped running, I did the complete opposite. I strolled gently through the meadow and it was simply stunning. I stepped out on to a gentle rise at the top to look at the view and just dropped in to standing meditation. I had one of the deepest meditations of my life there. Just standing. Sweat dripping off my nose, insects buzzing around and such wonderful understanding emerged. I touched awakening that day.

In many ways ease is the offset to diligence, and it reveals that step in the eight-fold path, right effort. We have to try, but not too hard. We must balance this out.

The Magic of Noticing – Andy Spragg

So many people these days are striving in their jobs and then having to go on stress management courses. It is a terrible thing that we need courses like that. Surely, we humans should know that we have to be gentle on ourselves and set time by?

Joy. When we think of joy, we think of happiness. But the two are different. Imagine you are incredibly thirsty. You have not drunk for days and someone hands you a glass of water. In that moment, that is joy! When you have drunk the water and are feeling better, that is happiness. Coming back to my experience in the meadow. There I was with a torn calf muscle, now late on my time for my run, but feeling immense joy as I stood in that meadow. We can develop joy just by paying attention! We should also take a joyful outlook on life. So many of us have a melancholy, pessimistic view of life. Some weeks ago, a friend had been on a holiday to Barbados. I asked her how she had got on. She poured out this story of how bad the flight had been, how she had spent three more hours than planned in the airport and how the taxi she had arranged had not turned up. That is what she relayed to me. A three-hour period of her holiday. I pushed her on the holiday itself. She said, "oh yes, that was fine thanks". Focus on the joy, otherwise you get eaten up by the bad stuff! When we widen our view outside of ourselves and our own stories, generally we find joy.

The sixth factor is concentration. There are of course many types of concentration. A thief, entering a house needs concentration. A sniper focussing on his target needs concentration. Even in the Buddha's day, there were many forms of concentration which took the individual away from themselves. Removing their ability to

The Magic of Noticing – Andy Spragg

connect with the world. So, we need to develop concentration that is wholesome. My best advice here is to go into the heart of suffering with your concentration. Look at the four noble truths and go into an understanding of these from your experience.

The seventh factor is equanimity, also sometimes known as letting go. As we said previously, all these branches of the tree grow together. They cannot be separated. By concentrating on and going into the nature of suffering, equanimity is revealed. What do we mean by equanimity? Well, essentially it is by paying equal attention to all things that we experience. We learn to embrace all aspects of our lives exactly as they are. We do not push things away. In this way we let go of our old habits of pushing away the bad stuff and grasping at the good stuff. This, we learn to understand, as the root of suffering. We practise this deeply, believe it or not, in Tai Chi when we concentrate on the yielding mind. As mentioned, I constantly work with the students on yielding. Here we find that in order to yield in the body we have to yield in the mind. Moments of conflict in our lives, therefore become opportunities to practise the yielding mind.

In our meditation, we can look to explore all of these factors. Even with mindfulness of breathing they all occur. Of course, we have mindfulness there, seeking to experience in our meditation, exactly what is. With interest we notice our mind overlaying concepts and thoughts and we strive to see through them. Our interest develops. In fact, we work to develop that enquiring mind to see into our experience. As we discover more both energy and joy develop, and we can see and experience even that progress with interest. We notice our effort. Whether we are striving to hard

The Magic of Noticing – Andy Spragg

or not enough and we apply mindfulness to see this. It is only with right effort that we will make progress. We apply that gentle nature of samadhi and we look into the nature of suffering in our meditation. Anywhere that we are blocking or pushing away experience, we will block progression. So, we learn equanimity in the meditation. The pain in our knee is just a part of the whole experience. We approach it with a sense of inclusion, friendship and acceptance.

8.5   Six element practice

Or alternatively, we could call this chapter - no self. In Buddhism one of the greatest challenges to get to grips with is this idea of no self. This is a huge subject and will be the subject of a later book. But I'm giving a short overview here.

Firstly, a little background in Buddhism that I think may help here. Buddhism is not a religion in the traditional sense. Although we don't refute the existence of a god or gods, we do not believe that we must rely on a god or other third party to make spiritual progress. We believe that we can make spiritual progress through our own efforts.

The Buddhist approach is very much a process. Through the practice of meditation and the eight-fold path we notice, we see directly and through this we change ourselves. One of the areas of change and key to progress is the perception of self. As we practise, we begin to see that there is no self. By this I mean nothing permanent about us that pervades through life and this leads to a deeper connection with the world and the people around us. It is a complex subject and also can be rather sensitive, with many of us believing in the concept of a permanent soul.

Buddhism is an art of experience rather than faith. So, we do not believe these things because the religion instructs us to. Rather, we set out to explore and find out for ourselves and it is this exploring that means we feel the teaching rather than trying to understand it on the cerebral level. So, we actively go searching for something such as the soul in our experience. As I say, controversial, so I'm not going to state here that there is no such thing as a soul. All I am saying is that it is the searching for things such as the soul, how we go about that search, that teaches us such a great deal about ourselves and our interaction with the world. It does not matter if we do not find the answer. Our answer, in terms of what we are looking to achieve in Buddhism, is revealed to us in the searching.

When we come to explore the idea of having no self, we have to explore every aspect of ourselves. We have to consider all of the elements that make us up. We can of course get very scientific about this these days, considering the atoms and molecules that make us. However, it is rather difficult to actually feel and differentiate between our atomic makeup! Fortunately, philosophy down the ages has given us a vehicle to help with this. We can consider ourselves from the perspective of the following elements: earth, air, fire (or heat or energy), water, space and consciousness. In our exploration we take each of these elements in turn and genuinely experience them in ourselves. Genuine experience is key here, so we rely on our five senses plus the experience of our mind to explore. As we move through each of these elements experiencing them in our bodies and the world

The Magic of Noticing – Andy Spragg

around us, we search for any permanent experience we can find. We try to find something that is permanent and that we can therefore call "me" or "I". Again, this is down in the experiential plane. This is very definitely not an academic exercise. We can use our memories though, to observe those elements that are perhaps a little less changeable than others. For example, the air element is constantly changing as we breathe in and out. But the earth element is present in our bones. We know our bones have changed, as we remember a time when we were much smaller, but we do not see much change, minute by minute. All this experience is poured into our meditation.

As we work through, we realise how difficult it is to find anything from our experience that can be described as permanent. Earth, air, fire, water and the space elements are all constantly changing, passing away and being created anew. As an example, the water element actually makes up 72% of our bodies. If there was any element that could stake a claim on contributing to a permanent entity called Andy Spragg, it would be my water element. It is certainly critical to my life. It is the glue that holds me together. Without water, I am just dust. But of course, we can see how ridiculous that is. The water that is in me today, fell from the sky a few weeks ago and I drank it in this morning. I will let it go again in a short time. It most definitely is not "me".

So, we come to consciousness - the mind and the sixth element. It is here that the meditation becomes very interesting. It is of course here that many people believe our identify or something of permanence resides. Are the conscious being and the soul synonymous for example?

The Magic of Noticing – Andy Spragg

Before we delve into this question though, let us take a look at where consciousness resides. The obvious answer to this is in our brain. Mind, brain and consciousness are often assumed to be the same thing. However, if we look at our own experiences, we quickly realise this is not quite right. Where do we feel our emotions for example? We do not feel them in our heads. We feel them usually in our heart area or our gut. Extreme emotions can even make our bones ache! In fact, modern biology tells us that our emotions are carried by neuropeptides which are manufactured and carried throughout our bodies. There is also a great deal of evidence to show a lot of the emotional content of our memories are buried deep within the cells of our bodies. It is this that allows us to connect with the whole human "beingness".

Science has recently even found neurons, the brain's messengers, in our gut. Our gut is literally our second brain!

Close your eyes and try to determine the size and extent of your mind. It's fascinating that it seems limitless. You can't find the edge of your mind. It is certainly bigger than your head and also your body.

As Buddhists we spend a great deal of time studying the nature of mind. Studying the nature of a thought, a memory, what drives our thoughts and what triggers the memories. Memories have a tendency to fade as we get older. Some are unreliable. Try to hold on to a memory in the mind. They are like gossamer slipping through the fingers. The same happens with thoughts; where do they come from and where do they go?

The Magic of Noticing – Andy Spragg

Spend a little time meditating and you soon discover how impermanent our conscious experience is.

So, where are we? Nowhere. What are we? Nothing.

But this cannot be right. This intuitively does not feel right and seems rather nihilistic. But it is our honest experience, that we cannot find anything permanent in our experience and we cannot find ourselves! This is a very good starting point from a Buddhist perspective.

In his book, 'The Ego Tunnel' Thomas Metzinger concludes that this emptiness is the way life actually is. Metzinger is a neuroscientist and not a Buddhist. But he draws the same conclusion, that our perception of self is an illusion created by the nature of our minds.

To the outsider coming to this, at first it seems rather pessimistic and actually rather disturbing. We are so firmly attached to the idea of self that letting go of this concept is extremely difficult. We cannot envisage a world where there is no 'me'. To the practising Buddhist, however, this perspective brings great comfort. As we have seen over previous chapters, at the heart of Buddhist teaching is this understanding that we all suffer, and much of our suffering is caused by our own desires and grasping approach to life. The ultimate desire of course is the desire to hang on to life. We want to remain healthy and young for ever. There is all manner of products out there that help us either to pretend to ourselves and others that we are retaining our youth or that make promises of extending life. However, never, in the history of man, has anyone cheated death.

The Magic of Noticing – Andy Spragg

From the perspective of no-self, the understanding is that we are simply the sum of parts. Of all the things that have happened before that culminate together at this instance in time and create this single moment of "Andy Spragg". Therefore, as there has never been a permanent entity called "Andy Spragg" there is no permanent entity to die. We will never die, as we were never born! This is key to really getting to grips with this concept and to anyone interested in this, I would encourage you to begin meditation and "feel" some of this. It really is an eye opener. With our "me" position we feel very much like a separate entity existing in the universe. Our desire to remain young and healthy and live forever grows out of our self-perception. What I am encouraging you to do here is to take a different perspective, that we are not separate. The elements that make us are not us, but are still very much a part of the Universe. They just happen to occupy the same space at a point in time.

When we start to experience this new perspective of no-self a huge feeling of connection with the people and the world around us arises. We are the elements that make us, and we connect deeply with everything around us.

In this way, as a Buddhist I constantly strive to let go of thoughts of self. Just directing my attention outward at the things I can feel, see, smell, taste and touch and also to experience the nature of mind and how it interrelates with these other senses. In this way, my connection deepens.

The meditation that is perfect for this is "just sitting", where we try to connect with some of this. In the meditation explore where you are and what you are, but stay with direct experience. Stay

The Magic of Noticing – Andy Spragg

away from expectations, desires, aversions and notice how the mind tries to pull you into the "I" place. This meditation requires strength of willpower and intent to not allow the mind to pull you into its personal agenda.

8.6   The law of conditionality

This is an area of Buddhist thinking which, on the surface, seems blindingly obvious but actually it turns out to be a very deep and powerful area of practice that we can explore in meditation.

Firstly, we can take a look at ourselves. Our basic values and views can tell us a great deal about the way we think and the way we view the world.

You might like to take a few minutes to really consider this question – "What do I believe is the purpose of life?"

This question cuts to the heart of spirituality and therefore is an excellent starting point to examine what it is that drives us. Because this is potentially such a driver in our lives it will also then influence the way we view the world.

In the current modern world, in the West, common thinking on religion and spirituality are disintegrating. Wind the clock back 100 years or so and the majority of the population were Christian in some way. But now we are left with a real melting pot of views in terms of spirituality. I think this is a good thing because it means we are not being pushed by the general society into particular religious beliefs. But there is of course one common value that is very much there these days: materialism. You could almost call it a spirituality because it brings us together in our thinking and provides a common ground. I almost wish I had not thought about and written it! We live in a society that is very materialistic, so we do need to look at this and see how it affects us when we answer this question.

The potential answer to this very large question - the purpose of life - covers a complete spectrum and we have many different approaches and religious views to draw on. As we consider our answer, we need to see where the answer comes from and how it makes us feel. We need to apply pure self-honesty to see what is driving our thinking. We need to look at the view we are choosing to see if it makes reasoned sense and what the likely consequences of the view might be in practice. For example, we may perhaps bring in our own personal fears, or even the fears and superstitions of our parents, and we need to examine our reaction to the view to see whether our choosing is based on superficial feelings or a real feeling of deep intuition. We will find that some views seem to constrain us and tie us down while others truly make us feel open and provide opportunity to expand our spiritual nature. This is more challenging than we probably expect.

The Buddha Said "Who is your enemy? Mind is your enemy. Who is your friend? Mind is your friend. Learn the ways of the mind. Tend the mind with care".

We have a story-telling mind and it can mislead us just as easily as another person. Once we learn this and we learn to not necessarily trust everything our minds tell us, then we start to make progress and trust the way the world is rather than what our mind is telling us.

As we get older this mind machine gets more complex. It populates the stories it tells us with even more complex and subtle arguments and beliefs. Take another look at the question we have asked here – "What do I believe is the purpose of life?". You have your view now and it is probably quite difficult to explain what it is; so many conflicting things come into play. We hear our mind saying "this is what my view SHOULD be" rather than what my view actually is.

Now spin yourself back to when you were five or six years old. Ask your younger self the same question. The answer is no doubt more pure, direct and heartfelt. It may be entirely different.

So, although it is important to think things through with logic. Actually, there are some questions that are best answered with pure awareness and intuition; the questions which do not seem to have a pure right and wrong and are very important to us. With these questions we must take great care that our mind is not misleading us. My advice here – USE MEDITATION! It can really help you. When faced with a challenge such as this, sit in meditation and just drop the question in to the subconscious mind. Work hard to not let conscious thinking take over. The more you practice, the easier this will get. Here we are working with the unconscious mind. We are allowing this to come forward. In Buddhist psychology – described in the Abhiddhama, we see two parts to the unconscious mind. The individual unconscious and the universal unconscious. With mindfulness we access and tap into both. Our individual unconscious contains our deep store of our beliefs, habits and fears. This has been filled through our lives, becoming more complex and intertwined. The universal conscious is a fascinating area. At first it sounds mystical and somehow esoteric. However, if we consider our physical bodies, it is fairly easy to understand that we are made up from the very elements around us, connected with them and constantly interchanging with them. If we consider that, then it is a small step to also consider the nature of mind. It is not just Buddhism that thinks this way. Ancient Greek thinking, the work of Bertrand Russell and even modern philosophy and neuroscience are exploring this. Take a look at Panpsychism if you get chance. The suggestion that consciousness may be universal in its scale. In this way, we are breaking out of the artificial shell that this sense of 'me' and 'I' creates.

Of course, when we connect with such a vast experience, things will come up that make absolutely no sense to us, because they are not emerging from our own experience. When these arise in meditation, we should just sit with them. Not try to push them away as irrelevant to us, but neither should we strive to logically understand them. Just soak them up as part of our experience. These experiences, the more we relax into them, may well help us to answer that key question "What do I believe is the purpose of life?". I advise caution though. At the same time, we need to balance this out with a healthy dose of scepticism to the things our own mind throws up. Remember the third root of suffering that the Buddha discovered – delusion. The veil of our own mind!

Do you have a friend who never lets you get a word in? Even when they ask you a question, before you have finished voicing your answer, they butt in and tell you their view. The individual

The Magic of Noticing – Andy Spragg

subconscious mind is like this. We need to give the universal subconscious a chance to speak to us.

So, where is this heading? Well, to a place where we are fully connected with everything around us, everything that has gone before and everything that is to come.

Buddha said "This being – That Becomes. From the arising of this – that arises. From this not becoming – that does not become. From the ceasing of this – that ceases".

This is a key aspect of Buddhist practice and a wonderful area for meditation and contemplation. It allows us to contemplate our place in the world and make spiritual progress.

There are two modes of conditionality or dependent arising, that the Buddha described. The first is purely circular and every single thing in this universe is subject to this. All things are subject to birth, life death and decay followed by new life. Even the very stones of our planet have gone through this.

Then, we have the second mode. This is the spiral mode. This holds the possibility real and permanent spiritual growth. This ONLY exists where the entity has self-awareness as it is this self-awareness that allows for the personal creative involvement.

Therefore, as humans, we have a choice. We can continue to function in the cyclic manner, or we can choose to act more creatively. Spiralling up, potentially, to full enlightenment.

Notice here that we are talking about conditions not causes. What is the difference? Well, think of a billiard ball that rolls across the table. We could argue that it rolls across the table because the cue hits it. That would be a cause. But we know that there are many more factors involved: the table surface and its nature, the weight of the ball, the viscosity of the air, even the mental state of the pool player. There are actually hundreds of millions of conditions all coming together to make that ball roll across the table and drop into the pocket.

Each and every time we step out of our front door there are 100 million conditions (meant to represent a large uncountable number) that affect our first step!

Cause is not the same as condition. A cause implies that if the cause happens, the effect will always happen. Conditionality is a vast flowing field of conditions all throughout the universe all contributing to our very next breath.

The body scan and just sitting are perfect meditations for exploring this. As we study and see each part of the body we can first of all exploring the constantly changing nature of the experience. Nothing is static. It is this constant change that results in life, but also in death. In the meditation we can get in touch deeply with the impermanence and fragility of the body.

Slowly through meditation in this way we see that everything is connected and dependent on everything else. See and understand that there is no separation. We are all deeply connected. Even those that have past continue to affect you deeply. The Buddha died some 2500 years ago but his thoughts and ideas are affecting us now. Read some poetry by Wordsworth and notice how his poetry still affects you now! The thoughts he was having when he wrote those words affects you. But you do not know him directly and he did not know you. But he is touching you and affecting you.

8.7   Karma - what is it?

Question. What do you think karma is?

The usual answer is that it is some sort of cosmic balance which influences our lives and always comes back to bite us. If you do bad stuff, then bad stuff happens. This view is closer to the traditional Indian Vedic view of Karma which is also present in the Hindu religion.

In Buddhism, it is a little different. Firstly, the word "karma" is translated as action. The result of our actions is what we call karma vipaka. In the previous chapter we looked at the Law of Conditionality or Dependent Arising.

Karma sits right in the heart of dependent arising, as far as our minds (and therefore our actions) are concerned.

Essentially, Buddhist thinking sees our minds as exhibiting mental habit. When certain situations arise, we fall into the ruts of our habitual mental behaviour and therefore, we always act in the same way.

Because of this, we always fall into the same traps. We are victims of our karma.

Note also here that the Buddha said that there are three things that can affect us in our lives. Natural events, other people's karma and our own karma. So, this is very much a departure from the traditional Vedic view because it means that stuff can happen to us which is either pure bad luck or good fortune. It is not always our fault! (As an aside, this is certainly a healthy view. In India for a while there was a behaviour, coming out of the Vedic view, of not giving money to charity to help those less fortunate, because those less fortunate people were atoning for previous actions and their karma should not be disturbed!)

So, we have karma, the action and karma vipaka, the result. Let us simplify this and simply call them karmic action and karmic result.

How do we bring this into our meditation? There are five constants of the mind. So, we have contact, feeling, interpretation, will and attention. Interpretation is key here as we notice how mental objects arise in the mind and the mind cuts in once the initial experience of the mental objects has happened and overlays other mental process and objects. It is a fascinating process and is very apparent when we meet new people. How we make all sorts of assumptions about them. Forming views of their status in life perhaps.

We can now look at all these constants and see and feel how karma interacts. Remember, by karma, we literally mean deep ingrained mental habit. Sitting in meditation we can experience the habitual nature of our minds and see how it leads us forward.

We can see how our encounter with the world goes through phases and those phases may be affected by our karma.

First phase, Contact. Contact is pure experience. There is very little involvement from our mind at this stage. Mainly it is subconscious. So, we can definitely say that this can only be karmic result. It isn't as a result of our own karma at this point because Mind is not involved. It is either as a result of our own previous actions, or from the actions of other people or from nature.

Second Phase, Mental Interpretation. This is primarily influenced by karmic result but there can be a certain amount of deliberate conscious interpretation at this point and therefore karmic action. Therefore, this is a good place to begin our mindful noticing in our examination of Karma. We can see the seeds of our mental habit if we pay attention. We can see how our subconscious rooted beliefs and prejudices perhaps bubble up and apply interpretation to the sense contact and influence our likes and dislikes.

Third Phase, Our own wilful intent. (Free will or maybe free won't?). If we are going to choose how we start to steer our karma vipaka, our karmic result, it is here where we go to work. Although our karma is in us, we can start to decide how we direct our thoughts. Unskilful thoughts arise in all of us, but through practising we can start to see how they build unskilful mental habit and therefore harm us. Ajahn Jutindharo, a Thai Forest monk and good friend, cites the importance of intent in our meditation. This is the vehicle for change.

Attention. This can be skilful or unskilful, so we have to take care with this one. As I have mentioned before, a sniper has a very concentrated type of attention, but I do not consider the practice to be very skilful from a spiritual perspective. So, will and attention go hand in hand as we direct our minds towards thoughts that are compassionate and skilful. Over time we will begin to notice how our responses to things change and therefore both our mental and our physical actions.

The meditation of metta practice or the metta bhavana (See 5.6), is excellent for developing our will and attention in the right direction, primarily to develop a sense of friendship and gentleness towards ourselves. We practise just sitting and experience self. See the nature of the subject. The complexity, the vulnerability. The impermanence. See the beauty. Watch when judgement arises. Notice that, relax into it and let it go. Each and every one of us has an infinite capacity for love and generosity. It is this that makes us so remarkable.

The Magic of Noticing – Andy Spragg

Chapter 9. Summary

The one common theme running through this book, and hence its title, is the magic of noticing. Through all my personal practice, I have found that this is so important to understand. We simply notice. We experience. We stay away from thought, we stay away from trying to figure things out. We just notice. With an open mind and an open heart. We notice the world around us and we notice what is going on inside of us. Even our mind, we just notice. Slowly, it is this noticing that has a transformational effect on us. We start to look beyond the veil of our own thoughts, judgements, prejudices and biases and see the world the way it is and see the way we react to things. It is this that leads us to the place where we change our reactions to the things that happen to us. It is this that leads to the easing of suffering in our lives.

But, remember this. It is our suffering that provides us with the remarkable capacity for empathy. Without suffering in our lives, we would have no empathy and therefore no compassion.

Strangely, although we have a desire to escape our suffering, it is that very suffering that gives us the seeds of compassion.

The Magic of Noticing – Andy Spragg

The Magic of Noticing – Andy Spragg

About the Author

Andy Spragg is a Practicing Buddhist and Tai Chi Teacher. Studying and practicing Buddhism since the early 90's he now runs The Sangha House with his wife Denise. A health and well-being and centre in Taunton, Somerset.

His passion is demonstrating that Buddhism is, very definitely, a spirituality for our modern age and takes his informal but informed teaching style into organisations and companies and also teaching people within the centre

www.thesanghahouse.co.uk
reception@thesanghahouse.co.uk
+44 1823 428156

The Magic of Noticing – Andy Spragg

Printed in Great Britain
by Amazon